DO MORE BETTER

Tim Challies
CRUCIFORM PRESS | DECEMBER 2015

Dedicated to Paul Martin,
the best kind of friend.

CruciformPress
ⓒCHALLIES

AUTHOR

Tim Challies is a Christian, a husband to Aileen, and a father to three children aged 9 to 15. He is a book reviewer for WORLD magazine, a co-founder of Cruciform Press, and has written several books including *The Discipline of Spiritual Discernment* and *Sexual Detox*. He worships and serves as a pastor at Grace Fellowship Church in Toronto, Ontario and writes daily at www.challies.com.

CruciformPress

Books of about 100 pages
Clear, inspiring, gospel-centered
CruciformPress.com

We like to keep it simple. So we publish short, clear, useful, inexpensive books for Christians and other curious people. Books that make sense and are easy to read, even as they tackle serious subjects.

We do this because the good news of Jesus Christ—the gospel—is the only thing that actually explains why this world is so wonderful and so awful all at the same time. Even better, the gospel applies to every single area of life, and offers real answers that aren't available from any other source.

These are books you can afford, enjoy, finish easily, benefit from, and remember. Check us out and see. Then join us as part of a publishing revolution that's good news for the gospel, the church, and the world.

TABLE OF CONTENTS

Do More Better: A Practical Guide to Productivity

Print / PDF ISBN: 978-1-941114-17-9
ePub ISBN: 978-1-941114-19-3
Mobipocket ISBN: 978-1-941114-18-6

INTRODUCTION

I believe this book can improve your life. This is a bold claim, I know, but the book would not be worth my time writing, or your time reading, if I did not believe it. I wrote this because I want you to do more better and because I believe you can. That is true whether you are a professional or a student, a pastor or a plumber, a work-from-home dad or a stay-at-home mom.

I don't want you to do more stuff or take on more projects or complete more tasks. Not necessarily. I don't want you to work longer hours or spend less time with your family and friends. I want you to do more good. I want you to do more of what matters most, and I want you to do it better. That's what I want for myself as well.

I wonder if you know that uncomfortable feeling that you are being neglectful toward at least some of life's responsibilities. I know it well. I recently caught an old episode of *The Ed Sullivan Show* and watched a plate spinner performing his act. He got the first plate spinning well, then moved on to a second and a third and a fourth and on down the line. Then he glanced over at the first and saw that it was just beginning to wobble. No sooner did he fix that one, then he had to dash back to the second, and back and forth and around in circles, all the while keeping a dozen plates spinning without crashing to the ground. Do you know that feeling in your life?

It does not have to be that way. It should not be that way. You—even you!—can live a calm and orderly life, sure of your responsibilities and confident in your progress. You can lay your head on your pillow at night and rest easy.

Thousands of years ago a man named Solomon, king of Israel, wrote these words:

> It is in vain that you rise up early
> > and go late to rest,
> eating the bread of anxious toil;
> > for he gives to his beloved sleep. (Psalm 127:2)

Even this king who ruled an entire nation, managed inconceivable wealth, and led spectacular building projects was able to free himself from stress and anxiety, to rest from his work, and to enjoy sweet slumber. So why do we find it so difficult with our little lives?

Over the years I have invested a lot of effort in understanding productivity and the skill of getting things done. I love to make the best use of my time and energy, and I am constantly fine-tuning the ideas, tools, and systems that help me to remain that way. From time to time I even get to teach these things to other people and to help them do more better. It is always a thrill to see them getting it and living it.

In this little book I will share some of what I have learned along the way because I believe it can help you learn more than you know now about living a productive life. That is not to say I have mastered it all. I am still learning and making small tweaks as I go. But I can say with confidence that what I will teach you really does work. It has brought order to my chaos and direction to my meandering. It has worked for many others as well.

The best way I know to teach these principles is to open up my life and to let you in a little bit. I will show you what I have learned, how I use my tools, how I build my systems, how I get stuff done. I think you will get the best value from this book if you read, observe, and imitate—at least at first. Then, as time goes on, you will inevitably adapt those tips you find especially helpful and discard the ones you do not. If I can spur your thinking so that you can do more better, I will consider this book a great success.

And now, to work!

ONE

KNOW YOUR PURPOSE

You may be reading this book because your life feels chaotic and you long to introduce some kind of order. You may be reading this book because you have taken on far too much and are looking for advice on what to prioritize. You may be reading it because you are always on the lookout for another tip or trick that can increase your efficiency just a little bit. Those are all good reasons and, no matter which of them fits you, I think you will find something here that can help.

But before we can get to the really practical stuff, you and I have a little bit of work to do. Even if you find yourself tempted to skip this chapter, I would ask you to resist that temptation. A small investment of time and attention right now will help build a foundation for all that will follow. If you skip ahead to chapter 5 or 6 and get right to the good stuff, you may be proving that you are looking for quick fixes rather than lasting change.

So stick with me as we do some important work in the chapter ahead.

THE FOUNDATION

No one has ever accused me of being handy. I can handle the very basics—hanging pictures or putting a coat of paint on the walls—but I am completely dependent upon my father-in-law or contractors to do much more than that. When I hear my friends talking about taping drywall, tinkering with pipes and wires, or installing doorways, I just slowly back away from the conversation. I know when I'm out of my league.

I haven't ever peered inside the walls of my home, but I know that if I did I would find beams and posts and pillars. And if I went downstairs to the basement and pulled off the drywall there, I would find a foundation. These are the elements that hold up my house and hold it together. The house cannot be stronger than these elements. What follows in this chapter is the foundation of productivity. Productivity—true productivity—will never be better or stronger than the foundation you build it upon. So let's make sure we are building upon a strong foundation.

A PRODUCTIVITY CATECHISM

An understanding of productivity needs to begin with an understanding of the reason you exist. Productivity is not what will bring purpose to your life, but what will enable you to excel in living out your existing purpose.

I am going to lead you through a brief Productivity Catechism, a series of questions and answers. Only when you understand these foundational matters about your God-given purpose and mission will you be ready to get to work. Here is the first question:

Q1. Ultimately, why did God create you?
A. God created me to bring glory to him.

This is the question every human being wonders at one time or another, isn't it? Why am I here? Why am I here instead of not here? Why did God create me? The Bible has an answer: "For from him and through him and to him are all things. To him be glory forever" (Romans 11:36). All things exist to bring glory to God, and that includes each one of us. That includes you.

God created you so he could receive glory from you and receive glory through you. That is an astonishing truth to consider and a deeply humbling one. When you grasp it and apply it, it transforms everything about your life. The simple fact is, you are not the point of your life. You are not the star of your show. If you live for yourself, your own comfort, your own glory, your own fame, you will miss out on your very purpose. God created you to bring glory to him.

Q2. How can you glorify God in your day-to-day life?
A. I can glorify God in my day-to-day life by doing good works.

You may be comfortable with this idea that God created you to bring glory to him, but the question remains: what does it actually mean to do that? If you want to glorify God, do you need to quit your job and become a pastor? If you want to glorify God, do you need to pack up everything you own, move across the world, and serve as a missionary in the farthest and most dangerous regions? Do you only truly glorify God on Sundays when you stand in church and sing the great songs of the Christian faith? Is God only honored through you when you read your Bible and pray? Or is there a way that you can glorify God all day and every day even in a very ordinary life?

Jesus answered this question when he said, "Let your light shine before others, so that they may see your good works and give glory to your Father who is in heaven" (Matthew 5:16). Your good works are like a light, and when that light shines, it illuminates God. When people see that light, they aren't meant to look at you and say, "He's incredible" or "She's amazing." They are meant to look at God and say, "He is awesome."

You do not glorify God only when you talk about him, or share his gospel with other people, or stand with hands raised in public worship. Those are all good actions, but they are not the only means through which you can bring glory to God. Far from it. You glorify God when you do good works. The apostle Peter wrote, "Keep your conduct among the Gentiles honorable, so that when they speak against you as evildoers, they may see your good deeds and glorify God on the day of visitation" (1 Peter 2:12). Your good works make God look great before a watching world.

Q3. What are good works?

A. Good works are deeds done for the glory of God and the benefit of other people.

You know now that good works are important and that they bring glory to God. But what are these good works? Are they feeding the poor and adopting orphans? Are they giving money to the church, volunteering at the food bank, or visiting the elderly in their nursing homes? What are the good works you are called to do? The Bible assures you that good works are any deeds that are done for the benefit of other people and the glory of God.

You are already very good at doing things that benefit you. We all are. From your infancy you have become adept at expending effort toward your own comfort and survival. But when God saved you, he gave you a heart that longs to do good for others. Suddenly you long to do good to other people, even at great cost to yourself. After all, that is exactly what Christ did on the cross. It is what Christ did, and he calls on you to imitate him.

Good works, then, are any and all of those deeds you do for the benefit of others. If you are a mother and you simply cuddle and comfort your crying child, you are doing a good work that glorifies God, because you do it for the benefit of your child. If you are a student and apply yourself to your studies, you are doing a good work that brings glory to God, because what you learn can and will be used someday to benefit other people. If you work in an office environment and do your job with consideration to your clients and coworkers, you are doing good works that bring glory to God, because you are living outside yourself, doing what benefits the people in your life.

There is no task in life that cannot be done for God's glory. Again, this is what Jesus calls for in these simple words from the Sermon on the Mount: "Let your light shine before others, so that they may see your good works and give glory to your Father who is in heaven" (Matthew 5:16).

Q4. But you are a sinful person. Can you actually do good works?

A.   Yes. Christians are able to do good works because of the finished work of Christ.

As a Christian you are aware of your sin. You know that your motives are never perfectly pure, that your desires are never perfectly selfless, that your actions are never perfectly just. Sometimes you do not even know your motives, and sometimes you do not even want to know them. If all of that is true, can you still do deeds that are good?

Yes, you can do good works. In fact, this is the very reason God saved you: "For we are his workmanship, created in Christ Jesus for good works, which God prepared beforehand, that we should walk in them" (Ephesians 2:10). It is simple: God saved you so that you could do good works and in that way bring glory to him. Paul amplifies it even more in his letter to Titus: "[Christ] gave himself for us to redeem us from all lawlessness and to purify for himself a people for his own possession who are zealous for good works" (Titus 2:14). Christ gave up his life for you so that you could have a genuine zeal to do good works. Paul calls upon Christians to be good works zealots or good works extremists—to be absolutely committed in every way to doing good for others.

Take heart! You can actually do works that delight God. God is genuinely pleased when you do these works, even when you don't do them as perfectly or as selflessly as you might wish, or even when you are uncertain about your motives. Though even your best deeds are far from perfect, God is pleased with them and accepts them with joy.

Q5. In what areas of life should you emphasize good works?

A. I ought to emphasize good works at all times and in all areas of life.

If you *can* bring glory to God in all areas, you *should* bring glory to God in all areas. There is no area of your life where you have no ability to do good to others and where you have no ability to bring glory to God. Paul said, "So, whether you eat or drink, or whatever you do, do all to the glory of God" (1 Corinthians 10:31). To Titus he said, "The saying is trustworthy, and I want you to insist on these things, so that those who have believed in God may be careful to devote themselves to good works. These things are excellent and profitable for people" (Titus 3:8). To Timothy he wrote specifically of women and said, "Women should adorn themselves…with what is proper for women who profess godliness—with good works" (1 Timothy 2:9-10), and to the church at Galatia he explained, "So then, as we have opportunity, let us do good to everyone, and especially to those who are of the household of faith" (Galatians 6:10). Peter even tells you that God has supernaturally gifted you so that you can do even more good to others.

> As each has received a gift, use it to serve one another,
> as good stewards of God's varied grace: whoever

speaks, as one who speaks oracles of God; whoever serves, as one who serves by the strength that God supplies—in order that in everything God may be glorified through Jesus Christ. To him belong glory and dominion forever and ever. Amen. (1 Peter 4:10-11)

The Bible is clear: At every time and in every context you are able to do good to others, and so you should do good to others.

Q6. What is productivity?
A. Productivity is effectively stewarding my gifts, talents, time, energy, and enthusiasm for the good of others and the glory of God.

Now we come to it: what is productivity? Productivity is *effectively stewarding your gifts, talents, time, energy, and enthusiasm for the good of others and the glory of God.* Productivity calls you to direct your whole life at this great goal of bringing glory to God by doing good for others. This call involves using your gifts, the spiritual gifts you were given when the Lord saved you; it involves deploying your talents, those areas of natural strength; it involves managing your time, those 24 hours God gives you each day; it involves making use of your energy, the strength or vitality that ebbs and flows through the day and the week; and it even involves your enthusiasm, the passion and interest you can bring to those works you love to do. God calls you to take all of that and to apply it carefully, faithfully, and consistently to the great goal of doing good to others.

YOUR PURPOSE

I trust this maxim establishes your purpose: to glorify God by doing good to others. There is no better plan and no higher ideal. So, ultimately, here is what productivity is all about and, therefore, what this book is all about: doing good to others.

Are you a stay-at-home mom? This is the measure of your productivity. Are you a CEO with a corner office? This is the measure of your productivity, too. Are you a teacher, a toolmaker, a doctor, a driver? The same is true of you. Even while we are talking about tools, software, and systems, you need to remember this high and noble purpose behind it all: bringing glory to God by doing good to others.

TWO

ANSWER THE CALL

Productivity is *effectively stewarding your gifts, talents, time, energy, and enthusiasm for the good of others and the glory of God.* This means you are responsible to take all you have and direct it to this one great goal. You are responsible before God to excel in productivity. And it should be simple, right? You just need to do the best thing (good to others) for the best goal (the glory of God). And yet, if you are like me and so many others, you have had a lifelong struggle to be and to remain productive. If your purpose is so clear, why do you struggle so much?

PRODUCTIVITY THIEVES

I am sure you can come up with a never-ending list of reasons that you are not more productive. But I believe lurking behind most of your reasons, and mine, we will find three main culprits, three productivity thieves: laziness, busyness, and the mean combination of thorns and thistles.

LAZINESS

The first productivity thief is laziness. You do not need to look far into the pages of the Bible to see that laziness has always been a concern. The book of Proverbs especially has a lot to say to and about the sluggard. In his little commentary on this big book, Derek Kidner points out that the sluggard is "a figure of tragi-comedy, with his sheer animal laziness (he is more than anchored to his bed: he is hinged to it, 26:14), his preposterous excuses ("there is a lion outside!" 26:13; 22:13) and his final helplessness."[1] As you study the sluggard throughout Proverbs you will see that he is a man who refuses to begin new ventures, a man who will not finish what he has begun, a man who will not face reality and, through it all, a man who is restless, helpless, and useless. His life is chaotic because his soul is chaotic. He cares little for God, so he cares little for those things that honor and glorify God—things like hard work and doing good for others.

There is something of the sluggard in most of us or perhaps in all of us—maybe even in you. If you want an excuse to be unproductive, you will inevitably find one, and if you can't find one, you will manufacture one. And it could be that today's world offers more ways of lazily procrastinating than ever before. When you ought to be working on your computer, you are only ever one or two clicks away from checking out your friends on Facebook or welcoming a few minutes of mindless entertainment on YouTube. Text messages provide a welcome distraction from deep thinking, and binge watching the latest series on Netflix can set you back a week. You are surrounded by temptations to laziness and may succumb far more often than you think. It could be that laziness is what stands between you and true productivity.

BUSYNESS

The second productivity thief is busyness. This is, of course, the very opposite of laziness—doing too much instead of doing too little. But it is no more noble a trait.

Busyness is a tricksy little fish. While it has undoubtedly always been a problem and a temptation, I do wonder if, again, we suffer from busy syndrome more today than we did in the past. After all, our society often judges us and ranks us according to our busyness. Although we complain about being busy, we also find that it validates us, as if we have only two choices before us: doing far too little or far too much. We somehow assume that our value is connected to our busyness.

But busyness cannot be confused with diligence. It cannot be confused with faithfulness or fruitfulness.[2] "Busyness does not mean you are a faithful or fruitful Christian. It only means you are busy, just like everyone else."[3] Busyness may make you feel good about yourself and give the illusion of getting things done, but it probably just means that you are directing too little attention in too many directions, that you are prioritizing all the wrong things, and that your productivity is suffering.

BUSYLAZY

What is both remarkable and absurd is that these two traits can even collide to form a kind of superstorm. In fact, one of the reasons I developed such a deep need and appreciation for productivity is that this combination is exactly what I saw in my own life. I am naturally lazy which means I am prone to ignore or procrastinate my responsibilities. That essay could wait a few more days, that book could sit there a bit longer, that bill hadn't come back with "final notice" yet, I could have that heart-to-heart with my daughter tomorrow. But eventually the bill came due and the essay needed to be handed in and my daughter just needed her daddy, and I went from lazy to frantic, from idle to crazy. The times of busyness would then make me so worn out that I would experience a crash and convince myself I had earned the right to lay low and be inactive for a little while.

THORNS & THISTLES

Busyness and laziness are both issues that arise from within. They are deficiencies in character that then work themselves out in our lives. And, as if they weren't already difficult enough, we also face challenges that come from outside ourselves.

God created us to live perfectly in a perfect world in which everything was working with us and for us. But then man rebelled against God and when he did that, God explained to him that there must be consequences. These consequences would extend all the way to work, to productivity. "Cursed is the ground because of you; in pain you shall eat of it all the days of your life; thorns and thistles it shall bring forth for you; and you shall eat the plants of the field" (Genesis 3:17b-18). The punishment was not work itself, but the difficulty that would now accompany work. What had once been easy would now be difficult. The ground that had once brought forth only good plants would now be a battleground between good plants and the thorns and thistles that would threaten to choke them out.

What is true for farming would also be true for every other job. Every task would face these "thorns and thistles," these difficulties that would constantly threaten productivity. And even today each one of us, no matter our vocation, has to grapple with them, to keep them at bay. The truck driver gets snarled in traffic, the doctor has patients who don't show up, the conference speaker misses his flight, the stay-at-home mom gets the call from school that her child has come down with flu and needs to come home.

THE ROOT PROBLEM

It could be busyness, it could be laziness, it could be the thorns and thistles, or it could be just about anything else, but whatever keeps you from doing good to others is a problem—a serious problem. It is a problem that keeps you from doing the very work God has called you to in the short time he gives you here on earth. Which means that the absence of productivity or the presence of woefully diminished productivity is first a theological problem. It is a failure to understand or apply the truths God reveals in the Bible.

Do you want to live in such a way that you do good to others and bring glory to God? Of course you do. Then what is it that keeps you from it? What is it that diminishes your productivity or steals it altogether? Whatever the answer is needs to be identified and rooted out. It needs to be destroyed and replaced for the good of others and the glory of God.

A CALL TO ACTION

This kind of true, biblical productivity calls you to action in all of life: You need to structure and organize your life so that you can do the maximum good for others and thus bring the maximum glory to God. Jesus calls you to let your light shine before others, and this light is more like a dimmer switch than a simple on and off button. You can reflect more or less of that light to shine before men. The more you let your light shine, the more others will see of your good deeds, and the more they will glorify God. You have the choice before you each day.

This truth means that productivity is not just about what you do in the workplace. It is not just about your success in the one task that consumes the greatest part of your time and attention each week. It is about all of life. It is about your personal life, your family life, your church life, and everything else.

A CALL TO CHARACTER

The kind of productivity I have described here is not only about what you do, but also about who you are. You need to be a certain kind of person before you can live this life.

What kind of person do you need to be? You need to be a Christian—a person who has believed in Jesus Christ and received forgiveness for your sins, a person who has given up living for yourself and begun living for the glory of God. If you have truly trusted in Christ, you will long to be like Christ, to put to death all the sin that is in you, and to come alive to all righteousness and holiness. You will long to do whatever it takes to make God look great.

God calls you to productivity, but he calls you to the right kind of productivity. He calls you to be productive for his sake, not your own. While this book will emphasize tools and systems and other important elements of productivity, nothing is more important than your own holiness and your own godliness. No amount of organization and time management will compensate for a lack of Christian character, not when it comes to this great calling of glory through good—bringing glory to God by doing good to others.

A CHALLENGE

I am glad that you want to emphasize productivity, but there is no great gain in being a productivity monster if the rest of your life is out of control. Productivity—doing good—has to extend to all of life, not just to one part of it. It has been widely shown, and it has been my experience, that there are certain habits and practices in life that are predictors to success in other areas of life. Displaying discipline and self-control in one area shores it up in others; conversely, neglecting discipline and self-control in any major area makes it all the more difficult to emphasize it in others. There can be a kind of chain reaction that leads to greater order or greater chaos.

Even if you are certain that greater productivity is the most pressing need in your life, I would encourage you to look wider and to choose at least one other major habit to emphasize at the same time. If you have been neglectful in your personal devotions, make that a habit you commit to. Exercise may be the most important and the most obvious of these habits and one that will improve just about every other area of life. Even while you pursue productivity, select another one or two habits to emphasize in parallel, and look for that chain reaction.

Action: Choose at least one habit other than productivity that you will pursue as you read and apply this book.

THREE

DEFINE YOUR RESPONSIBILITIES

Make no mistake: It is not easy to live in this world. We human beings are finite creatures who face infinite demands. There are so many things we *could* do in our lives and in any given moment, but so few we actually *can* do. There are fewer still we can do with excellence. So much of life involves attempting to strike the right balance between competing demands. We have families, churches, hobbies, and jobs, and all of them are competing for the same 168 hours we are given each week. Though time is so limited, the possibilities for using that time are unlimited. Productivity depends upon brokering peace between each of the different tasks we could prioritize in any given period of time.

As we get into the practical section of this book, I want to help bring peace to your life. The first steps down that path of peace involve doing an audit of your life. I will lead you as you look at your life through a kind of wide-angle lens, and together we will gather some important information. That is what we will do through the next several chapters.

I understand that this approach may not seem practical enough—you want to get straight to creating to-do lists and organizing information and completing tasks. We will get there, I promise. But not yet. I have tried the shortcuts and they never work in the end. Trust me and bear with me, and you will see that these chapters are as practical as anything that follows.

Action: Before you go any further, visit challies.com/ domorebetter and download the productivity worksheet.

AREAS OF RESPONSIBILITY

Each of us has areas for which we are responsible before God. We are all responsible for the care of our bodies and souls; parents are responsible for the physical and spiritual well-being of their children; husbands are responsible for providing for their wives, and fathers for their children; church members are responsible for extending love to the other members of the church; every Christian is responsible for caring for the poor and sharing the gospel. And this list is only scratching the surface. Such responsibilities can be overwhelming if we do not corral them and bring order to them.

Think about Jesus' parable of the talents in Matthew 25. Jesus describes a master going away on a journey and distributing his property to his servants for safekeeping. He entrusts different amounts to each of his servants, and then he leaves for a time. Two of the servants invest that money well and earn a tidy profit. The third servant, though, takes the safe route and buries his money in the ground.

And then the master returns. "Now after a long time the master of those servants came and settled accounts with them" (Matthew 25:19). Those who served as faithful stewards of their master's property are rewarded: "His master said to him, 'Well done, good and faithful servant. You have been faithful over a little; I will set you over much. Enter into the joy of your master'" (25:21, 23). The unfaithful servant, though, receives a terrible rebuke: "You wicked and slothful servant!" (25:26). The point is clear: God rewards those who faithfully steward what he has entrusted to them.

What is it that the Lord has entrusted to you? What has he made you responsible for? If the master gave talents to his servants and demanded an accounting, what has God given to you, and where will he demand that accounting?

I want you to create a list of each one of your areas of responsibility. You will need to think about all of life and create broad categories, asking the question: Before God, what am I responsible for?

Now here's the challenge: You need to have every one of life's responsibilities encompassed by a category, yet with as few categories as possible. I would suggest targeting five or six categories, with no more than nine.

Let me show you how I have done this thinking in my own life. I have structured my life into five areas of responsibility:

- Personal
- Family
- Church

- Social
- Business

There is no responsibility I have in life that falls outside of these five areas. If I am asked to be something or do something, if I am asked to dedicate time or attention to something, it will fit into one of them.

You will share some of these areas of responsibility, but you may have some different ones as well. You definitely have personal responsibilities—you need to care for your body and soul, and you need to clothe and feed yourself. You almost definitely have family responsibilities as well, whether they relate to a spouse and children, or parents and siblings, or all of the above. As a Christian you know that God has placed you in a local church community and charged you with all those New Testament "one another" commands, so you will also need a church area of responsibility. You have social responsibilities to be a committed friend and an evangelistic neighbor. You may be a student with school responsibilities, or a vice president with work responsibilities, or the organizer of a book club with hobby responsibilities.

My wife structures her life into her own five areas of responsibility:

- Personal
- Family
- Family Management
- Social
- Church

She chooses to divide family from family management, distinguishing the family members from the household management tasks.

A friend who is both a student and a full-time employee structures his life into six areas:

- Personal
- Family
- Church
- School
- Friends
- Work

Your list may perfectly match one of these, or it may only partially overlap. Each of us has different lives, so each of us has different areas of responsibility. *Vive la difference!*

 Action: Use the productivity worksheet to create a list of your areas of responsibility.

ROLES

Now that you have come up with those broad areas of responsibility, I want you to begin to bring greater definition to each of them. You will do so by listing the roles, tasks, or projects that fall under each.

Begin with your personal area of responsibility. What roles do you have there? What tasks has God given you? What projects are underway, or what projects would you like to begin? What are the criteria God may use when he requires that accounting? Begin to write those down as they come to mind, but do not be concerned if you miss some—you will be able to add to each list later on.

When you have finished with personal, move to family, and then go down the list until you have done the same for each area of responsibility.

I will illustrate by sharing a few of the roles that fall under some of my areas of responsibility and a few examples of what each of them includes.

AREA OF RESPONSIBILITY: PERSONAL

- *Spiritual fitness.* Spiritual fitness includes Scripture reading, prayer, church attendance, and reading good books.
- *Physical fitness.* I need to care for my body, so this area includes diet, exercise, and other elements.
- *Administration.* This area accounts for regular planning, reviewing, and other administrative tasks.

AREA OF RESPONSIBILITY: FAMILY

- *Spiritual care and leadership.* As a husband and father I am responsible to lead my wife and children and to care for their souls.
- *Home.* Though I am not at all handy, I still bear ultimate responsibility for ensuring that the home remains in good repair.
- *Financial care.* In the division of labor between my wife

and myself, I have taken on the financial care which involves our budget and the kids' allowances.

- *Family growth.* I plan our vacations and ensure we have regular family nights.

AREA OF RESPONSIBILITY: CHURCH

- *Elders' meetings.* This area includes responsibilities such as preparing and leading our meetings and ensuring that action items are completed.
- *Discipleship.* There are certain people in the church I meet with on a regular basis for discipleship purposes.
- *Members' meetings.* I typically organize and lead the church's regular members' meetings which involves preparing agendas, a short devotional, and serving as the meeting chair.
- *Pregnancy Care Center.* I am on the board of directors for a local pregnancy care center that is associated with our church, and this involves board meetings, committee responsibilities, and spiritual support.

As with your areas of responsibility, it is better to have fewer roles that encompass several items than to have hundreds of roles. Be as thorough as you can, but do know that this is a living list you will add to and take from on a regular basis.

Action: Using the productivity worksheet, list your roles, tasks, and projects within each of your areas of responsibility.

FOUR

STATE YOUR MISSION

You are already bringing a lot of order to your life through this simple audit. You have defined your areas of responsibility, and you now have a thorough list of many of the tasks, the roles, and the projects that fall under each one of them. You are off to a great start! And that means you are ready for your next assignment.

Think back to our definition of productivity: Productivity is *effectively stewarding your gifts, talents, time, energy, and enthusiasm for the good of others and the glory of God.* You have limited amounts of gifting, talents, time, energy, and enthusiasm, but unlimited ways of allocating them. For this reason productivity involves making decisions about how to allocate these finite resources. Many of these decisions involve saying either "yes" or "no"—"yes" to those responsibilities that appear to offer the best opportunity for you to do good to others and "no" to those responsibilities that appear to offer lesser opportunity for you to do good to others. These are very often difficult or even agonizing decisions to make. But these decisions are simplified when you know your mission.

MISSION

As Christians, we are on mission. Our mission is to do good to others and in that way to bring glory to God. That is our aim in the broadest sense, but we need to find ways of doing that mission in life's nitty-gritty. So what I want you to do now is to return to each of your areas of responsibility and to define your mission in each. After all, even with your roles and areas of responsibility all nicely laid out, you still have no means of knowing where you should invest effort and where you should not. Let me guide you through that.

DEFINE YOUR MISSION

I understand that defining your mission can sound very intimidating, so let me release the tension a little bit.

Many productivity gurus tell you that you need to have a personalized big-picture mission statement to encompass all of life and every area of responsibility. Personally, that both intimidates and paralyzes me, and I have never been successful at it. But what I have found very helpful is preparing a limited mission statement for each of my areas of responsibility. I have five areas of responsibility, and for that reason have five mission statements.

Let me release the tension a little more. My mission statements are not fixed and unchanging. Their primary purpose is to guide me week by week as I schedule my time and make decisions about where to expend effort. So while I do not change them haphazardly or without good reason, I do have freedom to tweak them as my mission comes into focus and as it changes throughout life. The primary value of seeing these as "living" statements is that it frees me from the paralysis of defining a mission that needs to guide me today and twenty years from now.

If you feel you will benefit from a whole-life mission statement, go ahead and create one. But at the very least, I want you to begin thinking about a mission statement for each of your areas of responsibility. You can come up with something today, and refine it over a period of days or weeks or even months.

Let me give you some examples of mission statements. Here are statements for three of my areas of responsibility: my work at the church, my business (which actually includes my ministry to the wider church and even this book!), and my personal life:

CHURCH

Teach, lead, and serve the people of Grace Fellowship Church as they mature and multiply.

Explanation: I believe that if the people of our church are living as Christians, they will mature in the faith, and they will multiply by sharing the gospel with others. My role in the church primarily involves teaching and training, both in formal and informal contexts; I want to do these things in such a way that it directs the people of the church to mature and multiply. All of this is captured in my brief mission statement.

BUSINESS

Use the opportunities God provides to help others think and live like mature Christians.

Explanation: Over the years, my core mission as a writer and public speaker has come into focus. What I love to do, and what I believe God has gifted me to do, is help people think and live like mature and maturing Christians. This is the focus of my blog, my books, and my public speaking—to help Christians grow and mature.

PERSONAL

Delight in God to the glory of God for the good of all people.

Explanation: I believe that if I am delighting in God, my delight brings glory to God and overflows into doing good for other people. I am a better father, a better husband, a better pastor, and a better neighbor when I am finding my delight in the Lord. In short, I am at my most productive when I am most delighting in God.

Each of these statements serves as a measure so that each week I can look back and ask, "Did I do these things?" And each of these statements serves as a call to action so I can look at the week ahead and ask, "How will I do these things?"

Action: Write a brief mission statement for each of your areas of responsibility. Give it your best shot for now, and prepare to keep refining them as time goes on.

ARE YOU ON MISSION?

Let's pause for a moment and consider where we have come. We have asked, "What are the things you are doing?" and, "What are the things you are responsible for?" We have then put together a mission for each one. But what we have not yet done is asked, "Are these the things you *should* be doing?"

What I want you to do now is to take a good look at those roles, tasks, and projects under each of your areas of responsibility and ask whether those are the things you ought to do. Do the things you do actually fit your mission?

Over time you inevitably collect roles, tasks, and projects that do not fit your mission. "In the same way that our closets get cluttered as clothes we never wear accumulate, so do our lives get cluttered as well-intended commitments and activities we've said yes to pile up. Most of these efforts didn't come with an expiration date."[4] Sometimes you accept tasks out of necessity—there is no one else to do it. Sometimes you accept projects out of mismanagement—the boss dumped it on you, and you had no ability to refuse. Sometimes you accept roles out of plain old fear of man—you were too afraid to say no, or you were too eager to impress others with your willingness to do it all. Or sometimes your mission has changed or come into sharper focus. But somehow our lives end up being like a junk drawer, stuffed full of things that don't belong anywhere else.

Your primary pursuit in productivity is not doing more things, but doing more good. Generally speaking, you can do more good for others if you have fewer roles and projects than if you have more. It is far better to dedicate lots of attention to those areas in which you are particularly talented or gifted than it is to dedicate minimal attention to the many areas you are not. "Only once you give yourself permission to stop trying to do it all, to stop saying yes to everyone, can you make your highest contribution towards the things that really matter."[5] What are those things that really matter in your life?

Randy Alcorn is one of many voices calling for planned neglect. He says,

> The key to a productive and contented life is "planned neglect"—knowing what not to do and being content with saying no to truly good, sometimes fantastic, opportunities. This happens only when you realize how truly limited you are, that you must steward your little life, and that of all the best things to do on the planet, God wants you to do only a miniscule number.[6]

You haven't begun to live a focused and productive life until you have said no to great opportunities that just do not fit your mission. There are many good things in this world that will go undone or that will have to be done by someone else.

So keeping your mission in mind, return to each one of your areas of responsibility, examine that list of roles and projects, and ask questions like these:

- Are these the right and best things for me to be doing?
- Do these things fit my mission?
- Are there things I can do in this area that no one else can do?

- Am I especially gifted or talented in this area?
- Do I bring unique value to this?
- Is there someone else who could do this better than I can?

I know that within my church I am constantly tempted to take on tasks or projects that would be better done by a deacon or an office administrator. Having these things done by a person better called, skilled, or equipped frees me to focus on my core mission. Yet as someone who loves the approval of others, I am tempted to take on tasks that are outside my core mission. In the end, they only end up being a great distraction from what matters most. I have needed to learn the slow "yes" and the quick "no."[7] My ability to make wise decisions is directly connected to my understanding of my mission. When I am confident in my mission, I am confident in my decisions.

Action: Look at each of the tasks, roles, and projects under each of your areas of responsibility and select the ones that do not fit your mission.

THE LEFTOVERS

At this point you may have a small collection of tasks, roles, and projects that do not fit your mission. You have several options for each of them:

You can *drop them*. You may find that certain things are being done for no good reason at all. For example, many churches have ministries that were started for valid purposes many years ago, but the ministry has long since become redundant or unnecessary. If it does not serve a clear purpose today, that time and energy would undoubtedly be better directed elsewhere. Just because that ministry or that project had a great past does not necessarily indicate it needs to have a future.

You can *delegate them* to someone who can do them better. Maybe you have been managing the family's budget, but you realize that your spouse can do it with greater skill or give it more substantial attention. Ask if he or she is willing to take on the task.

You can *do them*. Before you dump everything that doesn't perfectly fit your core mission, remember that your primary calling in life is to do good to others. This is where Christian productivity is unique. Most productivity gurus will encourage you to be as selfish as you need to be, to get rid of anything that doesn't interest or excite you. But as a Christian you know you can do things that do not perfectly fit your mission but still do them out of love for God and with a desire to glorify him.

God may call you to do things simply because they need to be done, and he will expect you to do them with joy and excellence. Who knows, he may even spiritually gift you to do them with the highest excellence. As Gene Edward Veith says,

> Essentially, your vocation is to be found in the place you occupy in the present. A person stuck in a dead-end job may have higher ambitions, but for the moment, that job, however humble, is his vocation. Flipping hamburgers, cleaning hotel rooms, emptying bedpans all have dignity as vocations, spheres of expressing love of neighbor through selfless service, in which God is masked.[8]

Action: Choose whether you will drop, delegate, or do each of those off-mission roles, tasks, or projects.

COMPLETING THE AUDIT

The audit is complete. You have gathered the information you need and are now almost ready to put all of that information to use. But before we can do that, we need to select your tools.

ASIDE: GOALS

Many books on productivity include a substantial section dealing with goals—the importance of goals, how to set good ones, and how to reach them. For some people goals are catalyzing, and for others they are paralyzing. Some people thrive with long-term and short-term goals, while other people never even consider setting, meeting, and beating goals. Personally, I consider goals a helpful but optional component of productivity.

Where goals can be especially helpful is in making mission practical. A mission is necessarily a broad and all-encompassing kind of statement, but it can be made more practical by establishing goals. Some goals may be very large and require a great deal of time to accomplish, while other goals may be very simple and easy to accomplish. Some goals are for a lifetime, while others are for a daytime. Both can have their place.

If you are the kind of person who thrives with goals, I would recommend fitting them in at this point—after defining your mission. Create goals that flow out of your areas of responsibility and that will help you succeed in your mission.

You can store these goals in the information management tool (chapter 8), meet the goals through a series of tasks (chapter 6), and set up a routine (chapter 10) to ensure that you regularly review them. While the kind of productivity system I outline in this book is not dependent upon goals, it is very capable of handling them.

FIVE

SELECT YOUR TOOLS

Tools are essentially human. At the dawn of human history, God created two people, naked and alone in a garden, and gave them a daunting task. They were to exercise dominion over the entire earth and to fill it with people (Genesis 1:28). They could be successful in this calling only if they developed tools appropriate to the task—plows to prepare the earth for crops, saws to cut wood for fuel, bridges to span the rivers. The first humans were completely dependent upon their tools, and since then each of us, in every area of life, has been dependent upon our tools. This includes you in your pursuit of productivity.

Because you are so dependent on your tools, there is every reason to ensure that you are using the best tools. A doctor can probably do surgery with a utility knife if he needs to, but you would prefer that he operates on you with a scalpel, and a very high-quality scalpel at that. You can go out in your backyard and cut down a tree with a crowbar, but you will get the job done better and faster if you use an axe. Yet many people try to be productive with tools that are poorly suited to the task.

You rely on tools to do work you cannot do yourself or to do tasks better than you could otherwise do them. When it comes to productivity, your tools are able to compensate for many of your shortcomings and do things you do not want to do yourself. You are bad at remembering mundane facts and information, yet completely dependent upon it—facts like your insurance policy number, flight schedule, or parking spot at the ball game. There are tools that are well suited to collect, archive, and access that kind of information for you. You are bad at remembering all of the tasks you need to accomplish in a day, which is why you may find yourself lying awake at night, trying desperately to remember all those tasks and deadlines due the next day and the next week. There are tools that can manage those items for you and present them to you just when you need them.

To a large degree, your productivity depends on identifying and using the best tools for the job and then growing in your skill in deploying them. This reality is no different from any other area of life. Preachers need to find and learn to use the best concordances and dictionaries and commentaries, and as they do so, they are able to preach better sermons. Musicians are constantly looking for finer instruments and always practicing so they can play them with more skill. Athletes fine tune their bodies and search for the best and latest equipment. And you, in your desire to be productive, will have to choose great tools and learn to use them well.

My focus will be on software tools—programs and services. Of course software necessitates hardware, but the hardware requirements are minimal: a basic laptop or desktop computer will do the job. A smartphone will be a great asset as well. The software I recommend will work on almost any computer platform or mobile phone.

3 ESSENTIAL TOOLS

Effective productivity depends upon three tools and the relationship between them.

- *Task management tool.* A task management tool enables you to capture and organize your projects and tasks.
- *Scheduling tool.* A scheduling tool enables you to organize your time and notifies you of pending events and appointments.
- *Information tool.* An information tool enables you to collect, archive, and access information.

Let me briefly describe these tools and provide recommendations for each.

The first essential tool is the one that is least familiar to most people: a task management tool. A task management tool enables you to capture and organize your projects, tasks, and actions. The older variant of this tool is a daytimer or a simple sheet of paper with a list of tasks to perform and a list of boxes to tick when those tasks are complete. Today there are excellent new programs that can manage all of your projects and tasks like never before.

I recommend Todoist (todoist.com) as your task management tool. Todoist will capture, organize, and display your projects and tasks while notifying you about the most urgent ones. It is accessible through a browser or through apps, which makes it accessible wherever you have a computer or mobile device. (Alternatives include Wunderlist, Asana, Things, OmniFocus, and many others.)

The second tool is for scheduling. A scheduling tool enables you to organize your time and notifies you of pending events and appointments. The older variant of this tool is the familiar calendar hanging on your wall or stuck with magnets to your refrigerator. Today there are electronic calendars that have most of the strengths of the paper calendar, but many additional powerful features such as the ability to notify or alert you before your events, or even to provide traffic alerts you may need to know about.

I recommend Google Calendar (calendar.google.com) as your scheduling tool. Google Calendar will hold and display all of your important events, meetings, and appointments and, through the notifications function, alert you ahead of any pending meetings or appointments. It is accessible through a web browser or many different apps, and this feature enables you to use it wherever you have a computer or mobile device.

Alternatives include Apple Calendar, Outlook, and a host of others.

The third essential took is an information tool. An information tool enables you to collect, archive, and access information. Not too long ago these were filing cabinets organized by folders, each of which held sheets of paper. It remains a familiar paradigm. Today, however, electronic information tools help you archive all (or most) of your information electronically, and this offers a host of important benefits such as universal access (you can access your files wherever you go) and searchability (with a few keystrokes you can search across your entire collection of information).

I recommend Evernote (evernote.com) as your information tool. Evernote is a powerful piece of software that enables you to capture almost any kind of information. Once information is captured, it is archived, indexed, and ready for future access. Evernote can install on nearly every bit of computer equipment you own and can be accessible wherever you have a computer or mobile device.

Alternatives include OneNote, Notability, and many others.

Action: Choose a scheduling tool, a task management tool, and an information tool.

AN ORGANIZING PRINCIPLE

Your productivity depends upon effectively and consistently using these three tools and upon effectively managing the interaction between them. At this point I am going to introduce an important organizing principle that you will return to again and again. This principle extends to any area of life but is especially helpful in organizing your productivity system. Here it is: *a home for everything, and like goes with like.*

Do not be deceived by the simplicity of this rule: It is a very, very powerful principle. If you were to consistently apply this principle all over your home or office, it would be and remain perfectly organized. You would never again find yourself scrambling to locate those items you tend to misplace. You would always know where your car keys are, because unless you were actually using them, they would remain in their home alongside all the other keys. You would always know where the extension cords are, because unless you were actually using them, they would remain in their home alongside the other extension cords.

When it comes to productivity, this principle is equally powerful. If you consistently apply it all over your life, your life will be and remain organized. You will never again find yourself lying awake wondering what important project you have forgotten about or where you left those important tax files. This principle tells you what to do with your information, what to do with your events, meetings, and appointments, and what to do with your tasks and projects. It tells you that appointments always need to go where appointments go, information always needs to go where information goes, and tasks always need to go where tasks go. It means that appointments and tasks should never be in the same place, and tasks and information should never be in the same place. Each of these things has a home, and it must always live there.

The principle can also be used in a more specific way. Multiple pieces of information that are alike need to be kept in the same place within your information tool. Several tasks that relate to the same project need to be kept in the same place in your task management tool. It tells you that all of the information about one area of responsibility needs be kept with the other information about that area of responsibility, and that all of your tasks related to one project need be kept with the other tasks related to that project.

Let that rule sink down deep, because you are soon going to be relying upon it.

TOOLS AND AREAS OF RESPONSIBILITY

You have selected your tools and learned the principle that will tell you when to use each of them. And now, at last, it is time to begin using those tools. Your tools function best when you combine them with a thorough understanding of your areas of responsibility. You will see as we begin to use our tools why I had you put so much effort into defining your responsibilities and roles.

SIX

COLLECT YOUR TASKS

The first tool you need to master is your task management tool. This tool represents the heart of an effective productivity system, and you will use it to store and organize your projects, tasks, and actions. While each of the three tools is important, none is more crucial to the functioning of the system than this one. In fact, there is a sense in which all of the other tools are supplemental to it, because this is the one that will determine and propel your actions each day.

Software-based task management tools are relatively new, so you may be far less familiar with them than with the other two essential tools. In the past, most people spread the functions of a task management tool across calendars, journals, scraps of paper, whiteboards, and email inboxes. Today, though, these tools bring new power and new capabilities to an age-old concern: getting things done.

I recommend Todoist as an exceptional tool for task management. It will be the software I use as I explain how to set up and use task management tools. If you have chosen to use another product, you should be able to follow the principles and extend them to your tool of choice.

To better organize tasks, Todoist offers various levels of structure or hierarchy. I recommend using three: projects, sub-projects, and tasks. Tasks (individual to-do items) go in subprojects (collections of related projects). Subprojects can be grouped into projects (collections of related subprojects). In other words, projects are composed of subprojects, and subprojects are composed of individual tasks. Don't worry if that is confusing, as I will explain it as we go.

Let's talk about how to get your life into a task management system and how to structure a basic workflow.

SETUP

Your first step is to visit todoist.com and create an account using your name and email address. You will probably find it easiest to do the initial setup within your browser on your desktop or laptop rather than using your mobile device. (Visit challies.com/domorebetter for more-detailed instructions.)

You are going to structure Todoist around your areas of responsibility. You will see that Todoist has several default projects already there: Shopping, Work, Errands, and so on. Delete all of them except the one called "Personal." Once all of the other projects are gone, turn your attention to the Personal project. You will configure it to contain all of the subprojects related to your personal areas of responsibility.

Now get out that productivity worksheet you filled out earlier. Look at the personal areas of responsibility and, in Todoist, click "+ Add Project" to create a project to correspond to one of the roles or projects for which you might want to collect tasks or action items. Type the name of the project, click the "indent" button to make it a subproject, and then click the "Add Project" button. Follow this pattern for each one of your personal roles or projects. When you are finished, you will see your personal project with all of your related subprojects neatly arranged underneath it. You may find it helpful to label subprojects with the name of the project, like this: Personal: Reading, Personal: Fitness, and so on.

Now go to each of your other areas of responsibility and do the same thing: Create a project for each of your areas of responsibility and create a subproject for each of the roles or projects for which you might want to collect tasks or action items.

Here are examples from my task management tool:

- Area of Responsibility: Family
  - Subproject: Finance
  - Subproject: Home
  - Subproject: Vacation
- Area of Responsibility: Business
  - Subproject: G3 Conference
  - Subproject: Visual Theology
  - Subproject: Finance
- Area of Responsibility: Church

- Subproject: Young Adults' Ministry
- Subproject: Members' Meetings
- Subproject: Pregnancy Care Center

Action: Create your projects and subprojects.

At this point you have as many projects as you do areas of responsibility, and under each of those projects you have a subproject to represent your projects, roles, or tasks. You are well on your way!

ADDING TASKS

Now that you have finished your Todoist setup, it is time to begin adding your tasks. There is only one thing you should ever add to Todoist: tasks. Tasks are specific and actionable items that relate to one of your projects. Whatever requires future action goes into your task management tool. And once again, your tasks need to adhere to the rule: *a home for everything, and like goes with like.* This approach means that all of your tasks related to family finance need to be together within that one subproject. All your tasks related to the church's preschool ministry need to be together within that subproject.

I recommend that you begin each of your tasks with a verb followed by a colon. This pattern brings at least two benefits. First, it ensures that you are only adding actions to Todoist and not using it as a place to hold information. Second, it makes it easy to skim your list of tasks to find ones that require the same kind of action (e.g. Buy, Write, Email, Call). After the verb and the colon add a brief description of the task (e.g. Buy:

New pens, Call: Pastor Bob, Send: Thank you note to Susan).

Here are examples from my task management tool:

- Area of Responsibility: Family
  - Subproject: Finance
    - Open: New savings account
    - Update: Budget
    - Research: New insurance policy
  - Subproject: Home
    - Register: Keurig
    - Complete: Kitchen paint
    - Buy: New fire extinguisher
- Area of Responsibility: Business
  - Subproject: G3 Conference
    - Decide: Text to preach
    - Prepare: Sermon
    - Book: Flights
  - Subproject: Visual Theology
    - Prepare: Marketing document
    - Complete: Chapter 3
    - Edit: Chapter 2
- Area of Responsibility: Church
  - Subproject: Young Adults' Ministry
    - Set: Next meeting date
    - Decide: Next meeting topic
    - Discuss: Future leadership

- Subproject: Members' Meetings
  - Create: Members' meeting agenda
  - Discuss: Agenda with elders
  - Send: Agenda to members

Action: Add some tasks to Todoist.

WORKFLOW

Now we need to consider a simple Todoist workflow.

Whenever you think of a task you must do in the future or would like to consider doing in the future, add it to Todoist. When you are in a meeting and a task or project is assigned to you, add it immediately. When you spot an item you need to fix or a product you need to buy, add a task to Todoist. Add tasks as soon as you think of them, and add them without restraint. Even if you are unsure if you will actually need to take action, add it now and make a decision about it later. Do not convince yourself that you will remember the task later that day or the next day. Whatever it is, get it out of your head and into Todoist.

Information you add to Todoist will automatically be added to your inbox. This inbox holds unfiltered and unsorted tasks, so you will need to process it on a regular basis. I recommend doing this step at least once each day either at the very beginning or very end of the day. I will describe a recommended daily routine in a later chapter. Processing your Todoist inbox involves briefly examining each note and making a decision about it. You have four options:

You can *delete it*. If it is a task you no longer need, delete it.

You can *do it*. If it is a task you can do immediately and one that will take no more than a few seconds, do it right now. The time and effort involved in filing it would be better spent simply completing it.

You can *defer it*. If it is a task you want to do at a future time, you will need to move it to the appropriate project and subproject. You may also wish to set a due date at this point. To do this, type something like "July 21" or "next Monday" in the "Schedule" box. If it is a task that happens on a recurring basis, you can add a recurring date, which will help you complete the task, but then have a new copy of it re-appear on a pre-determined schedule. To do this, type something like "every two weeks" or "every Thursday" in the "Schedule" box.

You can *delegate it*. If it is a task that needs to be completed but it would be best if someone else did it, delegate it to that person.

Do not stop processing your inbox until you have taken an appropriate action for *every one* of the tasks. The inbox is meant to be only a temporary holding spot for your tasks, so determine that you will never leave them there for long.

As you use your task management tool, there are two views that will need to receive most of your attention. All throughout the day you will need to consult your Today view which displays all of the tasks that are due today. The Next 7 Days view will alert you to any forthcoming due dates and deadlines.

As you accomplish tasks, mark them as complete and move

to the next one. Few things are more satisfying than clicking the "complete" button and watching that task disappear. You are getting things done!

Todoist and other task management tools require a small up-front investment in learning how to use them and how to best configure them. They require a small amount of ongoing maintenance. But they bring many tangible benefits. They are very powerful tools to propel action and to sustain it. However, like all tools, they require commitment. You will find that the more you use them and the better you use them, the better the results they provide. Do not give up too quickly!

NEXT STEPS

With the basic setup complete, consider searching for training videos that will teach you more about the ins and outs of Todoist. You can find several helpful tutorials that will show how others use the software and provide you with valuable tips.

Once you are comfortable with using Todoist on your desktop or laptop computer, consider installing it on your mobile device. This step will enable you to take your task list with you wherever you go and add tasks to it at any time, ensuring that no task is ever lost.

SEVEN

PLAN YOUR CALENDAR

With your tasks in their proper place, it is time to look to the third and final essential tool: your scheduling tool, or calendar. While there is still a lot of benefit in using a printed calendar, today's electronic calendars have added powerful new features such as sharing and notifications, and this addition makes them indispensable to productivity.

I have already recommended Google Calendar as a powerful calendaring tool and, as I proceed, I will explain how to set it up and how to use it. You are welcome to choose another calendaring tool and, while the particulars may vary, the general setup and usage should be very similar.

The degree to which you use your calendar and rely on your calendar will depend in large part on the particulars of your life. The more meetings and appointments you are responsible for, the more important it will be to put a lot of time and planning into your calendar. If you have very few timed appointments, your calendar can be far more basic and receive much less attention.

SETUP

Google Calendar can be accessed at calendar.google.com. If you do not have a Google account, go ahead and create one, and then sign in. And that's it. Setup really is that simple. Google does all the hard work for you, so all you need to do is use it.

However, you do have one decision to make. Google Calendar lets you have multiple calendars and you may find there is benefit to having one for each of your areas of responsibility. You need to determine whether you will have a single calendar that will encompass all of your areas of responsibility, or a separate calendar for each of them. The benefit of multiple calendars is the division between your areas of responsibility; the drawback is the added layer of complexity.

Action: Create your calendar and decide whether you want one calendar or several. Add a few upcoming meetings or appointments.

ORGANIZING YOUR CALENDAR

Once again we need to turn to the controlling principle of organization: *a home for everything, and like goes with like.* The calendar is the proper home for *something*, but for what? Let's talk about that.

The calendar is the proper home for events, meetings, and appointments. If you need to remember something that happens at a certain time or at a certain time and place, it is an ideal candidate for the calendar. These are the only items that belong on your calendar.

Let me give some examples from my own calendar:

- Monday at 11:00 a.m.: Workout at Health Club
- Tuesday at 6:30 a.m.: Men's Meeting at Grace Fellowship
- Wednesday at 7:00 p.m.: Midweek Prayer Meeting at Grace Fellowship Church
- Thursday at 2:00 p.m.: Phone call with Matthew
- Friday at 12:00 p.m.: Lunch with Drew at Swiss Chalet
- Saturday at 9:30 a.m.: Flight to Chicago at Pearson International Airport

Each of these items happens at a certain time or a certain time and place, and it is important that I remember to be where the event happens at the right time. These are the only items that belong on my calendar.

Putting *only* this information on your calendar may mark a significant shift for you. It is quite likely that in the past you have relied on your calendar as the home for your deadlines and tasks. However, we have already seen that task management software offers a far more effective solution. Once you have moved deadlines and tasks into their proper home, your calendar will be left with all of those events, meetings, and appointments—and hopefully nothing else.

WORKFLOW

Unlike task management, your calendar requires little workflow. You will simply add events, meetings, or appointments as you schedule them. As you add these items to your calendar, ensure that they have the proper date, time, and location information. In chapter 9 I will recommend a way of checking your calendar each day to ensure that you remain aware of all that is coming up.

However, the calendar does have one mission-critical daily function. When it is configured as I have outlined here— when it contains only events, meetings, and appointments—it provides important information that enables you to properly plan your day. As an important component of your daily review (another I will describe in chapter 9), you will begin each day by looking at your calendar to see how much time is committed to events, meetings, and appointments.

The time remaining is the time you can commit to completing tasks and moving forward with your projects. If you are in the office from 9:00 a.m. to 5:00 p.m., and have meetings from 9:00 a.m. to 11:00 a.m. and 1:00 p.m. to 1:30 p.m., a brief look at your calendar will give you a sense of how much time is available for tasks and projects, and you can then plan accordingly. If you are a stay-at-home mom and know that your child naps from 12:00 p.m. to 1:00 p.m. and that you need to pick up the other kids from school at 3:00 p.m., you will then have important information about when you can best plan to do the shopping, the tidying, and the phone call with the young lady you are mentoring.

USING NOTIFICATIONS

One of the great benefits of electronic calendars over their printed predecessors is that they have the ability to alert you to imminent events, meetings, or appointments. Google Calendar does so through what it calls notifications. These notifications will alert you through sounds and pop-ups on your computer or mobile device. They are tremendously helpful.

When you create a calendar event, be sure to set appropriate notifications. If you need to drive across town for an appointment, you may wish to set a notification 30 or 60 minutes before it begins. If have a meeting at 6:30 in the morning, you may wish to set an alert 12 hours in advance so you plan your bedtime and morning routine appropriately, and then another alert 90 minutes in advance to ensure you are on the road on time. Of course these notifications presuppose that you will have some kind of electronic device with you when the notifications occur. If this is not the case for you, you will need to find an alternate solution.

NEXT STEPS

The calendar is the most familiar of the three tools and, for that reason, the simplest to use. Once you have configured it on your desktop computer, consider adding it to your mobile devices as well. If you decided to use Google Calendar, this process should be straightforward on almost any device.

Most electronic calendars offer different ways to view your calendar: a monthly view, a weekly view, and sometimes a daily view. Consider appropriate times to use each of these views.

Consider sharing calendars among family members. Have one person in the family maintain the family calendar, and have each other member create their own calendar. Use Google Calendar's sharing function so every family member can see every other person's calendar.

EIGHT

GATHER YOUR INFORMATION

With your events and information in their proper place, you are now ready to consider your information management tool. As you know, this tool is used to collect, manage, and access information. It is the home for life's nouns—for the data, facts, documents, and information you may need to access in the future. It functions as your auxiliary brain.

I don't mean to disparage the brain. It's a remarkable organ and an outstanding evidence of the existence and wisdom of God. Yet the brain is limited in its capacity. Though the brain is perfectly capable of remembering much of life's mundane information, it is better to dedicate it to more important matters. Why focus on memorizing the details of that hotel reservation when you could put the effort into memorizing Scripture? Most of life's information can be added to your information tool. You can then trust this tool to remember it and to present it to you when you need it. This approach enables you to give your limited memory to only the most important facts and information.

I have already recommended Evernote as a powerful tool for information management, and as I proceed, I will explain how to set it up and use it. If you have chosen another product, you should still be able to follow the principles and set up your chosen tool in a similar fashion. It is less important that you use Evernote than that you use some kind of tool that can gather, store, and access your information, and do it in a logical, hierarchical fashion.

Evernote mimics a real world information-collecting system, and it offers three levels of hierarchy: notes, notebooks, and notebook stacks. Notes (individual pieces of information) go in notebooks (collections of related notes). Notebooks can be grouped into notebook stacks (collections of related notebooks). It is all very intuitive: Notes combine to make notebooks, and notebooks combine to make notebook stacks—just like pieces of paper in a binder, and binders on a bookshelf.

SETUP

Your first step is to visit evernote.com and download the software. I highly recommend doing the initial setup and configuration on a desktop or laptop computer rather than a mobile device. Once you have downloaded it, install and open it. Upon opening it, you will need to create an account using your email address.

By default Evernote has just two notebooks: First Notebook and Trash. Change the name "First Notebook" to "Inbox."

Next, get out the worksheet you used to define your areas

of responsibility. We are going to begin by creating a place for information related to your personal area of responsibility. We will create a notebook for each of the roles and tasks, then we will combine them together into a stack.

Take a look at your personal area of responsibility and create a notebook to correspond to each of the roles or projects for which you might want to collect and archive information. Once you have created those notebooks, combine them into a notebook stack and call the notebook stack "Personal." (Hint: Create a notebook stack by dragging one notebook on top of another notebook and then releasing it. Then drag all the other personal notebooks into that same stack.)

At this point you should have one notebook stack that contains all of your notebooks related to your personal area of responsibility, and two other individual notebooks: Inbox and Trash.

Now go to each of your other areas of responsibility and follow the same process: Create a notebook for each of the roles or projects for which you might want to collect and archive information, and combine them into notebook stacks.

If you find that you need to add more notebooks or notebook stacks than just your roles or projects, feel free to create them. However, try not to add them unnecessarily; whenever possible, have fewer rather than more. Do ensure that each notebook you create fits into one of your notebook stacks (with the exception of Inbox and Trash).

Here are examples from my own Evernote.

- Notebook Stack: Family
  - Notebook: Finance
  - Notebook: Vacation
  - Notebook: Spiritual Care
- Notebook Stack: Church
  - Notebook: Pregnancy Care Center
  - Notebook: Pastor's Toolbox
  - Notebook: Members' Meetings
- Notebook Stack: Personal
  - Notebook: Productivity
  - Notebook: General
  - Notebook: Physical Fitness

Each one of these notebooks corresponds to one of my roles, tasks, or projects.

This basic setup should take just a few minutes. By the end of this exercise you will have one notebook stack for each of your areas of responsibility, and each notebook stack will contain the notebooks related to that area. Besides that, you will have only those two other notebooks: Inbox and Trash.

Action: Create your notebooks and notebook stacks.

ORGANIZING EVERNOTE

One feature of Evernote that makes it especially powerful is its adaptability—there are many different ways to use it while still gaining a lot of benefit. There are two broad philosophies for organizing information within Evernote: using tags or using notebooks. Both have their strengths.

Notebooks enable you to find information by clicking through your hierarchy of notebook stacks, notebooks, and notes. In this way it is much like accessing information in a particular book by first going to the right bookcase, then selecting the right book, and then finding the right page. Tags, on the other hand, specialize in letting you find information by searching. In this way it is much like accessing information through a search engine such as Google. There is nothing wrong with exploring both options and determining which approach you prefer. You may find that one of them feels more intuitive or that one of them better fits the kind of information you need to add to Evernote. It does not really matter which of them you choose, but it does matter that you choose one of them and commit to it all the way.

I prefer to rely on notebooks and recommend it as the place to begin. However, I also add tags as supplementary data where it makes sense to do so. If you also prefer the notebook approach, you will want to ensure you add at least a small amount of information to every note you create.

- *You must:* Put each note inside a notebook.
- *You may:* Add a tag to each note.

Always ensure you follow the familiar dictum, *a home for everything, and like goes with like.* Also ensure that you do *something* with *everything.* There needs to be some way that every bit of information has a home and that every bit of information is stored with similar information. If you have twenty notes about a new car you are researching, put them all in the same notebook. If you have five notes about a forthcoming vacation, put them all in the same notebook.

ADDING INFORMATION

Now that you have configured Evernote, it is time to start feeding it your information, which Evernote refers to as notes. Evernote's strengths are capturing, archiving, and retrieving information—almost all kinds of information.

Evernote has powerful information-capturing capabilities. You can:

- Forward emails from your email account
- Use the mobile app to scan receipts or documents
- Use a scanner to scan and eliminate paperwork
- Use the mobile app to scan your handwritten meeting notes
- Use the microphone on your computer or mobile phone to record voice memos
- Use the web clipper to capture the content of any web page
- Use the web clipper to capture your Kindle notes and highlights
- Use your mobile phone's camera to add photographs
- Use your mobile phone's camera to capture your latest whiteboard session

- Use the Skitch app to capture information on your computer screen
- Drag Microsoft Word and Excel documents into Evernote
- Add pdf documents and highlight or annotate them from within Evernote

And that is just the start. Evernote can handle almost any kind of data. Once you feed that data into Evernote, it begins to process it, to add it to your personal search database, and to even scan it for keywords. Search within Evernote for "minutes" and it may even find that photograph of the notes you scrawled on the whiteboard during your last meeting.

Here are some examples from my own Evernote:

- Notebook Stack: Family
  - Notebook: Finance
    - Note: November credit card statement (a pdf file of my credit card statement)
    - Note: How to Get Maximum Value from Air Canada's Aeroplan Program (an article I clipped from a web site)
    - Note: Credit Report (a pdf containing my most recent credit score and report)
  - Notebook: Vacation
    - Note: The Best Day to Buy Airline Tickets (an article I clipped from a web site)
    - Note: Hotel Reservation (copy of a hotel confirmation for our forthcoming vacation)

- Note: Things to Do in Orlando (an email from a friend describing the best attractions in Orlando)

- Notebook Stack: Church
  - Notebook: Pregnancy Care Center
    - Note: PCC Board Meeting Minutes (a Word document sent by the board secretary)
    - Note: Complying with Anti-Spam Legislation (an article I clipped from a web site)
    - Note: This Year's Budget (an Excel spreadsheet)
  - Notebook: Pastor's Toolbox
    - Note: Put On, Put Off (a scanned document listing all of the put on and put off commandments of the New Testament)
    - Note: Initiating and Declining Sex in Marriage (a marriage-counseling article I clipped from a web site)

- Notebook Stack: Personal
  - Notebook: Productivity
    - Note: Charles Spurgeon on Punctuality (a long quote I copied and pasted from a website)
    - Note: Biblical Productivity by C.J. Mahaney (the pdf of C.J. Mahaney's excellent blog series on productivity)
    - Note: Productivity Worksheet (a pdf copy of a planning document I distribute when I speak on productivity)
    - Note: Random Thoughts (a voice recording of some unformed thoughts on productivity)

- Notebook: General
  - Note: John MacArthur's Library (a picture of my book *The Discipline of Spiritual Discernment* in John MacArthur's library)
  - Note: French Press (a pdf guide to making the perfect cup of coffee using a french press)

One of the principles you need to know about Evernote is that the more you commit to using it and the more information you add to it the more powerful it becomes. A half-hearted commitment provides halfway results, while a full-out commitment provides much more substantial results. Do not give up on it quickly and do not feel that you need to use it sparingly.

Action: Add some information to Evernote, ensuring that every note is filed appropriately.

WORKFLOW

Finally, we need to consider an Evernote workflow—the way to actually integrate it into your life.

Whenever you come across information that you may want to retain or remember, add it to Evernote. Use your desktop or laptop, use your mobile phone, use your tablet, or use your browser. Add information indiscriminately. Even if you are not certain whether it is actually information you will need to retain, add it now and defer the decision until later. Do not leave information you want to remember in your email inbox or your computer's downloads folder. Add it all to Evernote.

When you add information to Evernote, it will automatically be added to your inbox notebook. Because your inbox holds all those unfiltered and unsorted notes, you will need to access it on a regular basis in order to process everything. Do this at least once per week. Processing your Evernote inbox involves briefly examining each note and making a decision about it. You have only 2 options:

- *Trash it.* If it is information you no longer need, trash it.
- *Move it.* If it is information you want to keep, move it to an existing notebook or create a new notebook for it. Add any appropriate tags.

When you need to access information within Evernote, you can either click the appropriate notebook stack and notebook, or you can perform a search. Evernote's search function is very powerful and you will benefit from investing a little bit of time in learning how to use it well. The greater your familiarity with the search feature, the better you will become at quickly accessing your archived information.

NEXT STEPS

Once you have Evernote configured on your computer, consider ways to extend its functionality. Consider adding it to your (evernote.com/webclipper) so that you can quickly and easily add content from web pages.

The more you commit to Evernote, the more important security will become. Evernote offers strong protection and encryption, but one simple step can increase it all the more:

two-factor authentication. Two-factor authentication means that those who wish to access your account will need not only one security factor, such as your password, but also a second—typically your mobile phone. This step dramatically increases the difficulty they will experience in accessing your account.

Earlier you created mission statements for each of your areas of responsibility. Create a note and add each of those mission statements to it. Those statements will now live in Evernote.

Finally, consider searching for some of the Evernote training videos that are widely available on YouTube. You will also find a host of short, cheap, but helpful books on Amazon that will improve the way you use Evernote.

ASIDE: DOING GOOD

For four consecutive chapters we have focused on tools, looking at how to configure those tools and how to use them in daily life. Before we move on and consider how to get those three tools working in harmony with one another, I want to ensure we remember why we are doing all of this work. With our noses to the ground it would be easy to lose sight of the horizon, so let's elevate our gaze once again.

We are committed to productivity and to a distinctly Christian understanding of it. Productivity is *effectively stewarding your gifts, talents, time, energy, and enthusiasm for the good of others and the glory of God.* The reason we use these tools is that they enable us to be most effective in that calling. We are not working for our tools, but learning how to make our tools work for us. All we are doing in these chapters is meant to help us in our great pursuit of glorifying God by doing good to others.

NINE

LIVE
THE SYSTEM

If you take an honest look at your life, you will inevitably see times where you were highly motivated and times where you had almost no motivation at all. These times of high motivation usually come at New Years, when a new school year begins, or when your life undergoes a significant transition. In these times you love being organized, and you are able to live a structured life. For a while all goes well and productivity is easy and fun. But over time you get lazy, busy, or stressed out, and what was once fun becomes grueling. And before you know it you have gone right back to where you began. Why does this regress happen? Why does this pattern repeat itself?

Motivation, like the moon, waxes and wanes. At times it is full and bright; at times it seems hidden altogether. Motivation gives the desire and energy to begin making changes in your life, but it cannot sustain them. However, this does not mean you cannot be productive even when motivation is low. As many have pointed out, motivation gets you started, but habit keeps you going. You need to use those times of high motivation to build habits and to embed those habits in a system. That way, when motivation wanes, the system will keep you going.

THE POWER OF SYSTEM

Doing good to others and bringing glory to God is not something you can possibly think about every moment of every day, even though it is what you are called to every moment of every day. When you sit in your office doing paperwork, it is unlikely you will always ask, "How can I glorify God in this work?" When you take your child out for breakfast, you probably don't think, "How can I do him good and glorify God over the next hour?" Perhaps you should, and we undoubtedly all have a lot of room for growth.

But there is a solution, and the solution lies in systems. What is a system? A system is "a set of connected things or parts forming a complex whole."[14] A system has multiple parts that work together toward a common goal.

Imagine that you were tasked with building a railroad to transport goods from your town to one twenty miles away. You would need to construct a system, and the system would involve all kinds of components: tracks, switches, locomotives, boxcars, mechanisms to load the trains, signals to control traffic flow, and on and on. This system would be comprised of a complex collection of parts, but once it was constructed, it would work and function as a whole. If it was constructed well, it would function smoothly and efficiently.

But you do not need to build a railroad; you need to build a life of productivity—of doing good to others. And to do this work, you will need a system. A productivity system is a set of methods, habits, and routines that enable you to be most effective in knowing what to do and in actually doing it. An effective system involves identifying, deploying, and relying on appropriate tools. When functioning together, these tools enable you to operate smoothly and efficiently, dedicating appropriate time and attention to the most important tasks.

To be productive, you need a system. You need to build it, use it, perfect it, and rely on it. Your system needs to gain your confidence so that you can trust it to remember what needs to be remembered, to alert you to what is urgent, to direct you to what is important, and to divert you away from what is distracting.

Your system will ensure that you reserve moments of deliberate thoughtfulness where you will consider and plan how you can do good to others and in that way glorify God. You can structure your life and live within a system so that day by day and week by week you are executing plans and projects that reflect the time you have spent considering how to do those good things that bring glory to him.

3 TOOLS, 1 SYSTEM

You have selected your tools, configured them, and begun to use them. Now you need to construct the procedures that will enable you to use them together and depend on them. You need to make those tools work together in a simple but effective system.

Your tools work together to help plan your day, and your tools work together to help you get things done throughout your day. This reality means that your day needs to have two phases: planning and execution. In the planning phase you will make your plans for the day, and in the execution phase you will actually get your work done. While planning does not need to take much time, it is very important, and when done right, will dramatically increase what you are able to accomplish throughout the rest of the day.

Your tools have slightly different jobs during the planning and execution phases. During the planning phase, your scheduling tool shows you the time available in the day ahead, your task management tools tells you tasks available to you, and your information tool ensures that you have the necessary information. Then, during the execution phase, your scheduling tool notifies you of any pending events, meetings, or appointments, your task management tool tells you what to do, and your information tool provides the information you need to get those things done.

DAILY PLANNING

You have heard the old phrase: If you fail to plan, you plan to fail. If you plan nothing, it should come as no great surprise when you accomplish nothing. While there are times to plan strategically and far into the future, our first concern is for daily, tactical planning. An effective productivity system is absolutely dependent upon a short, daily planning phase that sets tasks into time and determines the items that will receive your attention in the day ahead.

CORAM DEO

To manage your day effectively you need to know what the possible tasks are for that day, what the necessary tasks are for that day, and what time is available to accomplish them. Once you have that information available, you can begin to fit tasks into your day like pieces in a puzzle—you set tasks into time. This is what you do during the daily planning phase. The purpose of this phase is to consider all of your projects, duties, and appointments, and to prayerfully choose the tasks that will receive your attention that day. To do so you will follow a routine that spreads out all of your possible tasks before you so you can choose the ones that you will attempt to complete.

The specifics of this routine will vary from person to person. I will lay out a routine below, suggesting that you use it as your starting point and then adapt it as you go. I call my daily planning phase my *coram Deo*, a Latin phrase that means *in the presence of God*, and I use this phrase because it helps remind me every day of whom it is I ultimately live for. R.C. Sproul explains its implications: "To live *coram Deo* is to live one's entire life in the presence of God, under the authority of God, to the glory of God."[15] The person who lives with an awareness of God's presence, who lives under God's authority, and who longs to bring God glory is the person who will be highly motivated to do more good—to do the most good for other people.

Action: Open Todoist and create a new project called Reviews (or you can call it Coram Deo). This project will not fall into any of your areas of responsibility, but will exist alongside them. Within the project add 6 tasks:

- [Get Focused] Pray
- [Get Clear] Bring: Task Inbox to o
- [Get Current] Check: Calendar & Alerts
- [Get Current] Check: Waiting for
- [Get Current] Check: Forecast for Next 7 days
- [Get Going] Choose: Today's top tasks

Set each task to repeat every day at or before the time you begin your workday. You can do so by clicking on the task and, where you see the words "no due date," simply type "every day at 6 am" or "daily at 9 am."

THE ROUTINE

At the start of your workday, before you do anything else, open Todoist and go to the Today screen to perform your daily review. Every day you will see those 6 tasks awaiting you and you will need to complete them all. As you complete them, you will see the due date change to the next day, indicating that the task has been completed and will need to be completed tomorrow as well.

Let me describe each of these tasks.

- [Get Focused] Pray
  - Purpose: Admit your dependence upon God and ask for his help.
  - Actions: Pause to pray just briefly, giving the day to the Lord and asking him to help you use it to his glory. Ask for wisdom to understand how you can best use your day to do good to others and ask for grace to do it well.

- [Get Clear] Bring: Task Inbox to o
  - Purpose: Ensure that every task has been properly assigned to a project.
  - Actions: Go to your Todoist inbox and process it by assigning any items there to a project. Delete, do, defer, or delegate every task. Whenever possible also assign a due date. Do not move to the next step in coram Deo until the inbox is empty.
- [Get Current] Check: Calendar & Alerts
  - Purposes: Ensure that you will not neglect any of today's events, appointments, or meetings, and gauge how much time is available for completing tasks.
  - Actions: Open your calendar and look for any meetings or appointments that are occurring today. Check each of them to ensure that you have set appropriate notifications. Make a note of how much time remains unaccounted for since this is time you have available to complete tasks.
- [Get Current] Check: Waiting for
  - Purpose: Determine whether you need to contact others today to discuss projects that are your responsibility, but for which they need to take the next action.
  - **Action:** Your productivity system needs to track items you have assigned to other people, but for which you are ultimately responsible. However you track those items, look to see if there are any that

have been completed or for which you need to send a reminder.

- [Get Current] Check: Forecast for Next 7 days
  - Purpose: Note any approaching deadlines.
  - Actions: Using the Next 7 days view, take a brief look at all due dates for the next 7 days. Make a note of any approaching deadlines.
- [Get Going] Choose: Today's top tasks
  - Purpose: Determine the tasks you will attempt to accomplish today.
  - **Action:** As you look at the Next 7 days view and as you consider those items you are waiting on, begin to decide the tasks you will attempt to accomplish today. Here is where you actually set tasks into time. Set the due date for these events to today. If you use Todoist's priority flags, you may set a priority flag as well.

This review is not a major commitment and takes only four or five minutes. However, that small investment pays great dividends. By the end of it, you will have looked at all the things you could do in the day ahead and have selected the ones you actually will do—or plan to do, at least. It is four or five minutes well invested.

DAILY EXECUTION

With the planning phase complete, you are now ready to execute. Your tools are now there to serve you—Todoist to tell you the options available to you, Evernote to provide the information you need to complete your tasks, and your calendar to remind you of any pending events, meetings, or appointments.

As you begin this phase, look at Todoist, choose a task, and begin to do it. And this is where my specific guidance will need to stop since your life and mine may be so different.

But even though I cannot tell you how to do your work or how to complete your tasks, I can offer some pointers.

USE ALL THREE TOOLS

You know our organizing principle: *a home for everything, and like goes with like.* In most cases it is quite simple to know how to distinguish between information, tasks, and events, but occasionally it is not quite so clear, especially when it comes to the distinction between tasks and events. Let's consider a few different items and see whether they belong on the calendar or in task management:

- *Doctor's appointment on Monday at 9 a.m.* This event goes on your calendar because it is an appointment that requires you to be at a specific place at a specific time.

- *Buy new pens.* This note goes in task management because it is an action, not an event, meeting, or appointment.

- *Open a new bank account.* This note goes in task management because it is an action. Even though there may eventually be a meeting associated with the action, for the time being it is a task.

- *Conference call on Wednesday at 4 p.m.* This event goes on your calendar because it is a meeting and requires you to be at a specific place at a specific time.
- *Book manuscript due.* This note goes in task management because it is a task or project, not an event, meeting, or appointment.

Those examples are all quite straightforward. Sometimes, though, you will need to create appointments on your calendar and tasks or projects in your task management software. Consider these examples:

- *Bible study.* You attend a weekly Bible study and are expected to lead the study once each month. You will create an event on your calendar called "Bible Study" for every Wednesday at 7 p.m. This step reminds you that you need to be at a certain place at a specific time. You will also create a task in your task management software called "Prepare: Bible Study" and set an appropriate due date. This action reminds you that you need to prepare for that meeting. The calendar ensures that you have marked off the time, and the task ensures you will prepare for it. You may also create a note in Evernote called Bible Study (filed in an appropriate notebook and notebook stack) where you will gather your ideas and material.
- *Preparing taxes.* You are responsible for mailing your tax information to the government and to do so you need to prepare material and then meet with your accountant. You will create an event on your calendar called

"Meeting with Accountant" for Thursday at 3 p.m. This step reminds you that you need to be at a certain place at a specific time. You will also create a task in your task management software called "Prepare: Tax Information" and set the due date for next Thursday. The calendar ensures that you have reserved the time to meet with the accountant, and the task ensures that you will be adequately prepared. Evernote may contain scanned copies of your receipts or your copy of last year's tax return.

KNOW YOURSELF

Getting things done is not only a matter of managing time, but also a matter of managing energy. In many vocations and in many places in life it is energy, not time, that is the more valuable commodity. Like time, energy is limited and needs to be used strategically. You can give massive amounts of time to certain areas of life, but if you only give those times in which your energy is at its lowest point, your productivity will still be low.

You need to know yourself. At what times of day are you at your mental peak? At what times of day are you least effective? Are you a morning person, a night-owl, or a mid-afternoon warrior? Plan to use your high-energy times to do your most important tasks. Try to schedule work that requires a lot of mental engagement at those times when your energy is high. This category includes creative work or possibly work that involves listening to people and engaging with them. Then try to schedule work that requires little mental engagement at those times that your energy is low. This category includes administrative tasks, running errands, and tidying your desk.

DO THE HARDEST TASKS FIRST

It is likely that you will begin most days with a list of several tasks, and you will have to choose which of them to begin with. It is equally likely that several of your tasks will be very simple and require only a few minutes to complete, while at least one other task will be daunting and take much longer to complete.

While it may be tempting to focus on several small tasks and reduce your task list substantially, there is often much more value in going straight after the hardest task. Accomplishing nine or ten low-priority tasks while neglecting the one high-priority task may make you feel better, but it is the very opposite of true productivity. Try to do the hardest thing first and when you're at your peak.

DO YOUR WORK FIRST

One of the great benefits of planning your day is that you will begin your day knowing the tasks that need to be prioritized. Try to complete these tasks before you start into the tasks other people may assign you. This advice may not fit every job and every work environment, but as Greg McKeown says, "If you don't prioritize your life, someone else will."[16]

EXPECT FAILURE

I know it sounds discouraging, but you will fail at times. Many days you will not get done all you need to get done. C.J.

Mahaney reminds us, "Only God gets his to-do list done each day."[17] The rest of us do what we can and some days come up short. If, at the end of the day, one of your tasks is undone, simply put it back into your system by changing the due date to tomorrow or to the next day you intend to work on it. Do not be discouraged by your inability to do it all.

REMEMBER YOUR PURPOSE

As you get things done, you will undoubtedly need to remind yourself again and again of your purpose. You do not exist in this world to get things done. You exist to glorify God by doing good to others. Remind yourself often of this important truth.

PRIORITIES AND INTERRUPTIONS

One of the common misconceptions about productivity is that productive and organized people always hit their deadlines, never have to request an extension, and never feel a crunch at the end of the week. But that is not the right way to measure productivity. Why? Because God is sovereign, and you are not. Even when you organize your life and plan your day, you will still have times when you fail and times you are overwhelmed. Your responsibility is to plan, organize, and execute to the best of your ability, but to realize that circumstances and providence may interrupt and delay even your best laid plans. Not only that, but you set and manage your priorities with the information available to you at the time, but this information is always limited.

Before we move on to our final chapter, let's look a little bit at priorities and interruptions.

CHOOSING PRIORITIES

We have established that every day there will be many things you *could* do, but only a few you *can* do. There will always be far more possibility than ability. Much of your productivity depends, then, on prioritization—on choosing the few and neglecting, ignoring, or even just plain refusing the many. This decision is often very difficult because there are so many good things to do and so many good opportunities you could take. Every author has a hundred more books he wishes he could write; every pastor has a hundred more meetings he wishes he could schedule; every mother has a hundred more conversations with her children that she would love to enjoy.

Let me offer four brief and simple tips on choosing priorities.

1. PLAN

It is important to plan. The planning phase and the weekly review (see the next chapter) are effective strategies for planning your priorities on both a macro and micro level. This planning often brings a great measure of clarity to your prioritization. C.J. Mahaney agrees: "My experience confirms that if I fail to attack my week with theologically informed planning, my week attacks me with an onslaught of the urgent. And I end up devoting more time to the urgent than the important."[18]

2. PRAY

It is important to pray. No, it is more than important. It is paramount. The Bible teaches that prayer is the means God uses to bring about his will so that as we pray, God acts. Prayer is an indispensable part of biblical productivity, because it causes us to acknowledge that God is sovereign over all of our plans, and it pleads with God to help us make wise and God-honoring decisions. The reason I begin my daily *coram Deo* with prayer is to ask God to help me identify and prioritize the most important tasks for the day ahead. And I believe he answers that prayer.

3. CONSIDER YOUR IDOLATRIES

Each of us is prone to seek satisfaction in someone or something other than God. As we consider priorities, we are wise to identify and to keep an eye on our idolatries, knowing that we will be prone to take on not the tasks that glorify God, but the tasks that validate us. Sinful men and women that we are, we may subtly assume that our top priorities should be those tasks that make us feel good about ourselves instead of actually doing good for others.

4. EMBRACE THE TENSION

It is important to understand that prioritizing effectively is more of an art than a science. There are always a few things that are undeniably high priorities and a few things that are undeniably low priorities. But the majority will fit somewhere in the middle, leaving you to make difficult decisions. These decisions are often more art than science, often requiring finesse and a best guess. Embrace the tension, because you will probably never quite solve it.

EXPECT INTERRUPTIONS

There is at least one unavoidable weakness to any productivity system: your inability to see the future. During the planning phase, you look at the day ahead and make a prediction about the future—you predict that you will have a certain number of hours available to you, and you plan how to use them. But your day may go in all kinds of unexpected directions. The pastor may have to make an unexpected hospital visit; the stay-at-home mom may have to pick up a sick child from school; the account manager may be summoned by his boss to an unplanned meeting. Suddenly your day has taken an unexpected turn and you did not even get a say in the matter.

In those interruptions you will face the temptation to react with anger or despair. But as a Christian who trusts in God's utter and absolute sovereignty over this world and all its affairs, you can react with joy, even when it seems impossible. God has his ways and his purposes, and it is futile to rebel against them. C.S. Lewis says this in his inimitable way:

> The great thing, if one can, is to stop regarding all the unpleasant things as interruptions of one's "own," or "real" life. The truth is of course that what one calls the interruptions are precisely one's real life—the life God is sending one day by day; what one calls one's "real life" is a phantom of one's own imagination.[19]

There is another kind of interruption—the interruption that requires you to make a decision about whether you will divert your time to a new task or a new project. The wife may be interrupted by her husband because he wants her help with a project, and she will need to decide how to respond. The employee may watch with dread as the boss walks into his office to ask if he would attend a meeting with a client, and he will need to make a decision about how to respond. As you make that decision, you walk a tightrope between two sins: fear of man and pride.

FEAR OF MAN

On the one side you will be tempted by fear of man, where pleasing other people is so important to you that you will be tempted to say yes to everything. You may respond this way because you love the other person's response when you say yes or because you dread the consequence of saying no. But either way, your fear of man may generate an inappropriate response that takes you away from better and higher priorities.

PRIDE

On the other side you will be tempted by pride. Pride may make you so convinced that you already know the best direction for your day that you will say no to everything, not letting even God himself interrupt your plans with something so much better than what you had plotted out.

Because your life is so prone to interruption and redirection, you have to hold to your plans loosely, trusting that God is both good and sovereign. At the same time, you cannot hold to your plans too loosely or you will be constantly sidetracked by less important matters. The solution is to approach each situation patiently and prayerfully and to trust that, in all things, God will be glorified so long as you flee from sin.

TEN

MAINTAIN IT CONSISTENTLY

Your system is now running smoothly, and day by day you are getting things done. But we haven't quite finished yet. One important matter remains.

You have probably noticed that there is nothing in this world that coasts toward order. There is nothing on all this sinful planet that, when left on its own, gets more orderly. Your productivity system is no exception. It needs consistent maintenance if it is to continue functioning smoothly. You need to free yourself from thinking that organizing your life is a one-shot deal. Far from it. Productivity is not a system you set up and then forget about, but something that demands dedicated attention on a regular basis. It is not something you configure one time and finalize, but something you need to constantly refine.

When you get in your car in the morning, I am sure you give the gauges a quick scan, even if that scan is largely subconscious. As soon as you start up the car, you check to make sure you have enough fuel to get where you are going, you take a glance to make sure the "check engine" light shuts off right on schedule, and you make certain there are no low-pressure warnings for your tires. But those quick scans of the gauges are not all you do to maintain your car. From time to time your car needs those more significant procedures like changing the oil and replacing the worn brake pads. In our little analogy, the daily scan of the gauges is much like your daily planning or *coram Deo*—it is deliberately limited in its scope and purpose. In this chapter we want to discuss the more significant maintenance—the productivity equivalent of replacing the oil and adjusting the brakes. That is what you do in your weekly review.

THE POWER OF CHECKLISTS

I would like to offer one simple but effective way you can guard against the creep of chaos and disorder while maintaining the consistency and integrity of your system.

My friend Steve is a pilot, and many times each week he climbs into the cockpit of an airliner to prepare to take two hundred people several miles into the sky. While flying sounds like it ought to be a terrifying and dangerous thing to do, it is actually very safe—far safer than most other modes of travel. Why is that? There are many reasons, of course, but one of the most significant is that pilots are trained to follow very specific procedures from the moment they step into the cockpit to the moment they step out. These procedures ensure that the pilots verify that every part of the plane is functioning just as it is meant to and that they have set every setting, pressed every button, and tuned every dial in exactly the right way and the right order. Flying a plane is a very complicated procedure, and there is far more to it than a pilot can easily retain in his brain. For that reason pilots rely on a simple tool that is ideally suited to help them remember everything they need to do: a checklist.

Your life is undoubtedly complicated and there is far more to it than you can easily retain in your brain. In many cases it is wise to outsource some of the thoughts you need to remember to that very same tool. I have found no better way of maintaining my system than to work through a short checklist each week. This list helps me ensure that the system is functioning properly. It calls me back to the system when I have drifted and it takes care of the routine maintenance that ensures each part is working just as it should. This checklist is what I call my weekly review.

SERVE AND SURPRISE

Before we turn to that weekly review, I want to introduce you to one very helpful paradigm.

We have established that you have several areas of responsibility and, within each of them, a list of roles. These are roles and responsibilities entrusted to you by God. This reality means that he defines your success or failure.

As you step back to think about each of those areas of responsibility, how can you think well about succeeding and excelling in each of them? I have found no better way than this helpful paradigm: serve and surprise.[20] To succeed as a husband I need to serve my wife, and to excel as a husband I need to surprise my wife. To succeed as a local church elder I need to serve my church, and to excel as an elder I need to surprise my church. Let me explain that a little more.

As Christians we are called to serve God by serving others. We are slaves or servants of God and are called to imitate Jesus Christ who joyfully served us in the costliest and most significant way. In his letter to the Philippians, Paul says,

> Let each of you look not only to his own interests, but also to the interests of others. Have this mind among yourselves, which is yours in Christ Jesus, who, though he was in the form of God, did not count equality with God a thing to be grasped, but emptied himself taking the form of a servant, being born in the likeness of men. And being found in human form, he humbled himself by becoming obedient to the point of death, even death on a cross. (Philippians 2:4-8)

We are to look out for the interests of others—to serve others. And why do we do so? Because we want to be like Christ who served us by leaving his Father's side, by becoming human, by living on this sinful planet, by suffering a terrible death, and by facing the wrath of God for sin. If Christ has served us to such a great extent, who are we to withhold even the smallest act of service from one another?

As we think about living a productive life, *serve* answers this question: What must I do this week? What are the things I must do in the week ahead in order to be faithful to what God has called me to in each of my areas of responsibility? What will it look like for me to be a faithful pastor in the week ahead? What must I do to be an effective husband to my wife? What does God say I must do with and to and for my children in order to be a godly and loving father to them?

Serving is beautiful, but we can do better than that. Serving represents those things we must do, but we can also surprise. *Surprise* answers this question: What can I do this week? What can I do to excel in this role God has given me? What are the things I could do this week to surprise and delight my children? What are things I could say or gifts I could give that would be an unexpected blessing to the people of my church? How can I serve as a faithful image of the God who delights to give good gifts to his children (Matthew 7:11)?

That is what we are called to in each of our areas of responsibility: to serve and surprise. So as we turn to our weekly checklist, we will work toward this question: How can I serve and surprise in the week ahead?

THE WEEKLY REVIEW

Your daily planning session is meant to be tactical: It has a limited purpose and a narrow scope. But where the daily planning is tactical, a weekly review offers a chance to be more strategic, to widen the scope and the purpose. This review offers the opportunity to set new plans into motion, to restart projects that have stalled, and to course-correct plans that are drifting. Where the daily *coram Deo* takes only a couple of minutes, the weekly review requires a little bit more time—I find that I need to block off around 30 minutes for it. I schedule it for each Friday afternoon so that when a new week begins on Sunday, it is already planned and organized.

This weekly review is a work in progress and I occasionally add a step or remove a step. But on the whole it is comprised of these actions:

- [Get Focused] Pray
- [Get Clear] Bring: Email Inbox to o
- [Get Clear] Bring: Evernote Inbox to o
- [Get Clear] Bring: Task Inbox to o
- [Get Clear] Tidy: Desk
- [Get Clear] Tidy: Desktop
- [Get Current] Review: Calendar for next 30 days
- [Get Current] Review: Evernote notebooks
- [Get Current] Review: All projects
- [Get Current] Review: Next 7 days
- [Get Set] Review: Mission
- [Get Focused] Plan: Serve and surprise
- [Get Going] Decide: Next week's deadlines, deliverables, and priorities

As with *coram Deo*, I suggest you begin by copying my weekly routine, then add to it and take from it as you go.

Here is a brief overview of what to do in each step.

- [Get Focused] Pray. Pray briefly, asking God to give you wisdom to understand the possibilities for the week ahead and to give you wisdom to know which of them most merit your attention.

- [Get Clear] Bring: Email Inbox to o. [Get Clear] Bring: Evernote Inbox to o. [Get Clear] Bring: Task Inbox to o. Tidy up all three of your inboxes to ensure that your system is clean and running smoothly. All emails need to be replied to or filed (see the bonus chapter at the end of this book), all information in Evernote needs to be placed in its proper notebook, and all tasks need to be filed in their appropriate projects. If you have a physical inbox on or near your desktop, clean it up as well.

- [Get Clear] Tidy: Desk. Clean up your physical workspace, filing any papers, putting away any books that have accumulated, and so on. Put everything in its home. Consider extending this step a little bit beyond your desk to any other place that paper, books, or other bits and pieces tend to accumulate. You do not need to do a total cleaning of your office, but you should gather anything that could contain information that may be helpful as you plan the week ahead.

- [Get Clear] Tidy: Desktop. Clear up any files that have ended up on your computer's desktop. If you use a downloads folder, clean that up as well. Wherever files accumulate, go there, and either delete them or move them to their proper home.

By the time these [Get Clear] steps are complete, every-thing is where it ought to be as per the familiar rule: *a home for everything, and like goes with like.* Now that you are clear, you can work on getting current. You are going to look at your tools to familiarize yourself with all the items you could take action on in the week ahead.

- [Get Current] Review: Calendar for next 30 days. Look over your calendar to see if there are any major events coming up that you ought to be aware of. Because I rarely need to take action on work that is more than 30 days ahead, a month is plenty of time for me, but you may find that you need to adjust that number to encompass more or less time.

- [Get Current] Review: Evernote notebooks. There are certain notebooks in Evernote that may contain crucial information and that ought to be regularly reviewed. These notebooks will vary for each one of us according to the particulars of our lives, but an example might be an account manager who has a notebook containing infor-mation about each of his clients. At the end of the week, it would be wise for him to go through that notebook to see if there are any notes that have not been updated in a long time (which would indicate that he has not been in touch with that client for a long time) or any notes that contain time-sensitive information (which would indicate that he may need to take actions next week). Where he sees that kind of information, he should then create tasks to check in with those clients or to take other appropriate actions.

If you have mission-critical notebooks like those, make them part of your weekly review project. You do not need to review all of your notebooks, but only the few that contain especially important or actionable information.

- [Get Current] Review: All projects. Now it is time to review every single one of the projects in your task management system (which, as you know, are marked as subprojects in Todoist). This is a step you will be tempted to skip, but do not skip it. I can hardly overstate the importance of this step for the functioning of your system. At least once a week, lay eyes on every one of your projects. It involves taking a glance at each of your projects to look for a few important pieces of information:

  - Does that project have at least one task in it? Are there any tasks to add?

  - Does that project have any tasks within it that have been completed but not marked as complete?

  - Does that project have a pending deadline that you need to be aware of for next week?

  - Is there anything else that needs to be added to or adjusted within the project?

- [Get Current] Review: Next 7 days. Open the Next 7 days screen in Todoist and take a look at everything that is due in the next 7 days. Look especially for those high-importance tasks, projects, or deadlines that may be sneaking up on you.

At the end of these [Get Current] steps you have gathered

all the information you need to make wise and informed decisions about the week ahead. You now know all of the tasks you *could* take action on in the week ahead. However, you still need to make the decisions about which you will actually attempt to complete. However, there is one step before that.

- [Get Set] Review: Mission. Go to Evernote where you keep that list of mission statements for each of your areas of responsibility. Read each one of those mission statements. Try to read them slowly and meditatively rather than in a perfunctory way. If you would like to make some minor tweaks to your mission statements, do so now.

At the end of [Get Set] you have put everything in its place, gotten all the information you need, and reminded yourself of your mission. Now, at last, you can get going.

- [Get Focused] Plan: Serve and surprise. Consider each of your areas of responsibility and ask, "How can I serve and surprise in the week ahead?" Consider what it means to be faithful in this area, and then consider what you can do to surprise and delight over the next 7 days. As you do so, create the appropriate tasks with appropriate due dates. For example, you may realize that there are basic areas of service where you ought to improve—you have gotten lax in family devotions ("Schedule: Family devotions") or it has been too long since you have financially supported the church ("Write: Check for the church"). You may get creative with ways to surprise others—providing an unexpected gift for your wife ("Buy: Flowers for Aileen") or support to that person in your church who is going through a difficult time ("Write: Card to Aaron"). Visit challies.com/domore-better to download a weekly Serve & Surprise worksheet.

- [Get Going] Decide: Next week's deadlines, deliverables, and priorities. At the end of it all, decide what you mean to focus on in the next week or weeks. As you do so, assign due dates as appropriate. Here is an example: In my review of the Evening Service project, I see that I will be preaching the next part of my series on the following Sunday evening. Therefore I set the due date on that task for Friday. Next week Tuesday, when I do my daily *coram Deo* and look 7 days ahead, I will see it as an option for that day and flag it as one of that day's top tasks.

MAINTAIN IT

This weekly review will soon become a fundamental part of your productivity system. Your system will function well when you make time for this review and it will begin to sputter when you do not. Of course, a strong system will be able to endure brief times of neglect—we all have a bad week or need to take some vacation, and missing a single weekly review will not harm the system too badly. But missing several of them in a row will eventually cause a significant weakening. Dustin Wax says it well:

No matter how organized you are, how together your system is, how careful you are about processing your inbox, making a task list, and working your calendar, if you don't stop every now and again to look at the "big picture," you're going to get overwhelmed. You end up simply responding to what's thrown at you, instead of proactively creating the conditions of your life.[21]

Find a time for your weekly review, add it to your calendar, and commit to doing it every week. I really can't over-emphasize the importance of this discipline.

A CLOSING WORD

Thank you for reading and for listening. It has been my prayer in preparing this book that it would help spur you on to the love and good deeds that God calls us to (Hebrews 10:24). As humans created in God's image, and as Christians saved by God's grace, we have a remarkable privilege. We have the joy and the responsibility of stewarding our gifts, talents, time, energy, and enthusiasm for the good of others and the glory of God. This is your privilege and this is your purpose. So go and do. Do more better.

TAME YOUR EMAIL

6 TIPS FOR DOING MORE BETTER WITH EMAIL

I think most of us have a love-hate relationship with email. On the one hand it brings many benefits—it delivers news, encouragement from friends, and fun notes from family members. It also has immense practical value—it delivers confirmation that the ticket order went through or that the book we want is on sale. But, of course, there is a dark side: the endless spam, the discussions that go on for far too long, the newsletters we didn't sign up for, and the chain letters promising bad luck if we don't forward them to twenty other people. Email has become a mess of function and dysfunction. We need it, yet we hate it.

DOING EMAIL BADLY

To better understand why so many of us do email so badly, let's draw a comparison to a real-world object: your mailbox. Imagine if you treated your actual, physical mailbox like you treat your email. Here's how it would go.

You walk outside to check your mail and reach into your mailbox. Sure enough, you've got some new mail. You take out one of your letters, open it up, and begin to read it. You get about halfway through, realize it is not that interesting, stuff it back inside the envelope, and put it back in the mailbox muttering "I'll deal with this one later." You open the next letter and find that it is a little bit more interesting, but you do the same thing—stuff it back into the envelope and put it back inside the mailbox. Other mail you pull out and don't even bother reading—it just goes straight back inside the mailbox. And sure enough, your mailbox is soon crammed full of a combination of hundreds of unopened and unread letters plus hundreds of opened and read or partially read letters.

But it gets worse. You don't just use your mailbox to receive and hold letters, but also to track your calendar items. You reach in deep and pull out a handful of papers with important dates and events written on them, including a few that have come and gone without you even noticing or remembering. And, of course, you also use your mailbox as a task list, so you've got all kinds of post-it notes in there with your to-do items scrawled all over them.

But we aren't done yet. Even though you feel guilty and kind of sick every time you open your mailbox, you still find yourself checking your mail constantly. Fifty or sixty times a day you stop whatever else you are doing, you venture down the driveway, and reach your hand inside to see if there is anything new.

It is absurd, right? Your life would be total chaos. And yet that is exactly how most people treat their email. It is chaotic, with no rules or procedures to control it. What do you need? You need a system.

DOING EMAIL BETTER

We once again need to consider our foundational principle of organization: *a home for everything, and like goes with like.* On a high level, we now know that events, meetings, and appointments belong in our calendar; tasks and projects belong in our task management software; and information belongs in our information management tool. That leaves email as the place for communication—communication and nothing else. Email is an abysmal task management tool and a woefully poor scheduling tool. It is tolerable only if we make it do what it does passably well: communication.

We can also use that principle of organization on a more granular level. Here it tells us that our email inbox is the place for unprocessed email and for nothing else. The inbox is not the proper home for archived email or for email that is awaiting our reply.

You need to build a simple system that will enable you to tame your inbox. Your email system can be as simple or as complex as you want, but the simplest method of all involves just four locations: a place to receive new email, a place to hold email you will reply to at a later time, a place to hold email you need to keep for archive purposes, and a trash bin for all the rest. It really can be that simple.

The inbox is the place to receive email. No matter what email program you use, your inbox will be built-in and probably already full of email. You also need a place to temporarily hold email as it waits for your reply, so go ahead and create a folder or label called Reply. You need a place to hold email that you will be keeping for archive purposes. Most email programs already have this functionality as well. If your program does not, create a folder or label called Archive. And, finally, you will need the built-in trash bin or Delete folder.

With our folders in place, let's put together a workflow.

EMAIL WORKFLOW

Open your inbox and begin with the very first email. Open it up and immediately decide what you will do with it. You have a few options:

- *Trash it.* If it is junk or something that is irrelevant to you, erase it.
- *Archive it.* If it is something you may need in the future, but requires no action on your part, archive it. (That may mean sending it to your Archive folder or it may mean forwarding it to Evernote.)
- *Reply to it.* If you can reply to it in no more than ten or fifteen seconds and with little mental exertion, do so right away.
- *Move it to your Reply folder.* If you cannot reply to it in just a few seconds or if it will require some thought or prior actions, move it to your Reply folder.

Now move to the next email in your inbox, and then the one after that, and the one after that. Do not skip emails and do not allow yourself to do nothing with any of your emails. By the time you are finished, you should have zero emails in your inbox.

When all of your email is processed and your inbox is empty, you have two options: Close down your email and move on to something else, or go into your Reply folder and begin to reply to those emails.

In general, and if your job lets you, it is best to check email occasionally rather than constantly. Whenever you check it, process everything in your inbox until the inbox is empty.

Let me give some pointers about working with email and your other tools:

- When an email requires complicated actions before you can reply to it, you may want to archive or even delete the email and add a task to your task management software. Once you have accomplished the task or project through your task management software, you can find that email again and reply to it or just begin a new one.

- When an email contains particularly important information, consider adding it to your information management tool. If you use Evernote, they have assigned you an email address. You can forward email to this address and it will show up in your Evernote inbox. Do this with any information that you would like to be able to search for in Evernote.

- When an email contains an event, meeting, or appointment, immediately add that to your calendar and then archive or delete the email.

This method relies on using your email program's search functionality to find archived email, so the more powerful the search, the more successful it will be. For that reason I typically recommend Gmail as a superior email program.

This email system is very effective, but it will depend upon your commitment. If you commit to the system, train yourself to master it, and form it as a new habit, it will permanently transform and improve your relationship with email.

20 TIPS TO INCREASE YOUR PRODUCTIVITY

Here are twenty tips to increase your productivity.

1. *Be curious.* When you meet someone who appears to be especially productive or organized, ask him or her for tips. I have learned a lot by reading great books, but even more by asking others how they manage their time, how they built a system, and how they have learned to be successful in their tasks.

2. *Plan to recite and remember.* Use your task management software to remind you to review things you have memorized. I love to memorize Scripture and poetry and have my software set to remind me each day to review a different poem or Bible passage. This habit ensures that they remain fresh in my mind.

3. *Break it down.* Be careful of tasks that are dauntingly huge. "Write: A Great Novel" is so giant a task you may never begin, and even if you do, you will be unable to

track your progress. Break giant tasks into a series of smaller tasks and work through them progressively.

4. *Use a password manager.* We all have a lot of passwords to remember today—passwords for email and Facebook and banking and just about everything else. A password manager can be a very helpful tool. Begin by going online and searching for 1Password or LastPass. These programs will help you remember your passwords while also increasing the strength of your passwords.

5. *Use strong passwords.* A bad password is, well, bad. You make a criminal's life exponentially more difficult if you determine you will use stronger and better passwords. There is much debate as to what constitutes a good password, but whatever else you believe, a good password is one that protects your account and one that you can actually remember. I recommend using four random words strung together. This kind of password is more memorable than a random string of letters, numbers, and punctuation marks and actually offers better protection. A mnemonic device, perhaps a silly little scenario that uses all four words, can help you remember your new password.

6. *Create a not-to-do list.* Create a note within Evernote that will contain a not-to-do list. Make this a list of bad productivity habits you are trying to break, and go over this list each week during your weekly review. My not-to-do list includes "Do not drink coffee after 2 p.m.," "Do not leave email open all day," and "Do not agree to

meetings that have no agenda or no end-time."

7. *Set a time-limit on meetings.* Meetings tend to expand to fill the time you give them. You will probably find that you can get as much done in a short and focused meeting as in a long and unfocused one. Be sure that all participants know when the meeting begins and when it ends. Begin on time and end on time.

8. *Prioritize personal devotions.* Productivity is fueled by the spiritual disciplines. You are not truly productive if you get things done all day while neglecting your soul. Be careful that your personal devotions do not become just another item to check off your to-do list.

9. *Stop multi-tasking.* Multi-tasking is rarely effective and almost never leads to increased productivity. Whenever possible choose a task, take it to completion, and then move on to the next one.

10. *Move around.* Sometimes a change of scenery is as good as time off. If you are doing creative work, try bouncing from coffee shop to coffee shop, switching every couple of hours. If you usually work from the kitchen table, try switching to a different room for a few hours. The quiet room at the local library is one of my favorite places to hole up for a couple of hours of writing.

11. *Learn to delegate.* Delegation is a rare skill, but refusing to delegate can rob you of time you could spend doing the most important things. Think creatively about who may be able to handle some of the tasks that keep you from getting other things accomplished. What may be

drudgery to you may be a joy to someone else. What you do poorly someone else may be able to do with excellence.

12. *Track your time.* Every now and again it may be helpful to audit your use of time. You can do this manually by simply recording start and stop times in a journal or automatically by using software tools such as Toggl or RescueTime. Auditing your time will show you when and where you are most efficient productive while also showing you when and where you tend to waste time.

13. *Don't leave email open.* Set aside specific times in the day when you will check email, and keep it closed at all other times. Most of us can make do very well even if we check only once or twice in a day.

14. *Plan to rest.* Plan to take at least one day out of every week where you rest from as many responsibilities as you can. If you do not plan this day it will soon get away from you, so plan when it will be and plan how you will use it.

15. *Turn off notifications.* Whenever possible turn off notifications on your electronic devices. You probably do not need to be notified every time you receive an email or every time your friends update Facebook. Fight against the distraction that seems to grow with every new generation of software and devices.

16. *Write it down.* If you don't write it down you will probably forget it. Most of us live with the dread that many of our best ideas are forever lost because we forgot to write them down. As soon as you have an idea, get it into Evernote. You may forget, but Evernote doesn't.

17. *Take breaks.* Breaks may seem like lost productivity, but they actually enhance your productivity. Schedule breaks into your day and enjoy them guilt-free. The busier your day, the more important they will be. So get up for a few minutes, walk around the block, get hot (if your workplace is cold) or cold (if your workplace is hot), grab a cup of coffee, and get back into it.

18. *Get accountability.* Have someone check in with you on a regular basis (perhaps during a team meeting) to ask if you are keeping up with your productivity system. Having something or someone outside the system prompting you to maintain the system will help keep you going when motivation is low.

19. *Don't send unnecessary email.* Sending unnecessary email means you will also receive unnecessary email. Send sparingly and you will receive sparingly.

20. *Exercise.* I know it seems counterintuitive, but sometimes the best thing you can do for productivity is to stop trying to be so productive and to spend some time exercising. Productivity is about all of life and requires all of your body and mind. Make sure you make time to get fit and to stay fit.

ENDNOTES

1. Derek Kidner, *Proverbs* (Downers Grove, IL: IVP Academic, 1964), 42-43.
2. C.J. Mahaney, *Biblical Productivity* (Sovereign Grace Ministries, 2010), 1-6.
3. Kevin DeYoung, *Crazy Busy* (Wheaton, IL: Crossway, 2013), 32.
4. Greg McKeown, *Essentialism* (New York, NY: Crown Business, 2014), location 234.
5. McKeown, *Essentialism*, location 83.
6. Randy Alcorn, "A Lesson Hard Learned: Being Content with Saying No to Truly Good Opportunities," (November 10, 2014), *Eternal Perspective Ministries*, accessed November 5, 2015, http://www.epm.org/blog/2014/Nov/10/saying-no.
7. McKeown, *Essentialism*, location 1603.
8. Gene Edward Veith, *The Spirituality of the Cross* (Concordia Publishing: St. Louis, MO, 1999), 80.
9. Tremper Longman, *Proverbs* (Grand Rapids, MI: Baker Academic, 2006), 297.
10. Ibid, 297.
11. Kidner, *Proverbs*, 100.
12. Eric Lane, *Proverbs: Everyday Wisdom for Everyone.* (Great Britain: Christian Focus Publications, 2000).
13. Ibid.
14. Angus Stevenson and Christine A. Lindberg, ed., *New Oxford American Dictionary* (New York: Oxford University Press, 2010), "System."
15. R.C. Sproul, "What Does 'coram Deo' Mean?", May 27, 2015, *Ligonier Ministries*, accessed November 5, 2015, http://www.ligonier.org/blog/what-does-coram-deo-mean/.
16. Greg McKeown, "If You Don't Prioritize Your Life Someone Else Will," November 13, 2014, *GregMcKeown.com*, accessed November 5, 2015, http://gregmckeown.com/blog/if-you-dont-prioritize-your-life-someone-else-will-harvard-business-review-2/.
17. Mahaney, *Biblical Productivity*, 36.
18. Mahaney, *Biblical Productivity*, 13.
19. C.S. Lewis, *The Quotable Lewis* (Wheaton, IL: Tyndale House Publishers, 1989), 335. As quoted in Mahaney, *Biblical Productivity*, 34.
20. Mahaney, *Biblical Productivity*, 28.
21. Dustin Wax, "Back to Basics: Your Weekly Review," *Lifehack*, accessed November 5, 2015, http://bit.ly/1LsRWM3.